Inside:

ARCHIVES

Vol 10 • First Edition • Lublin 2019

ISBN: 978-83-66148-00-0

Editor-in-chief: Damian Majsak
Assistant editor: Kamil Stopiński
Translation/Proof-reading: T. Basarabowicz
e-mail: redakcja@kagero.pl
phone +4881 501-21-05
DTP: Kagero Studio

Editorial board reserves the right to shorten texts and changing of titles and also is not responsible for author's opinions contained in texts. Non ordered materials will not be returned.

Publisher:
KAGERO Publishing
Akacjowa 100, Turka, os. Borek,
20-258 Lublin 62, Poland
www.kagero.pl, kagero@kagero.pl

Marketing:
Joanna Majsak marketing@kagero.pl

Sales: e-mail: oferta@kagero.pl,
phone/fax +4881 501-21-05

The "Hollands" From Vancouver

Story of the AG type submarines in the Russian and Soviet Navy

Jan Radziemski

Hull of an AG type submarine on the slipway of the Baltic Shipyard

Introduction

Submarines of the AG type belonged to one of the most numerous of World War One. Designed by a company belonging to the well-known constructor Holland, they were built in the USA and then in Britain. Their assembly was carried out by shipyards in Canada and Russia. A total of 71 ships of this type were built, out of this number 35 served in the Royal Navy, 8 in the Italian fleet, 11 in Russian and 9 in the US Navy (including 6 ships not collected by tsarist Russia). After the war, two ships were handed over to Canada by the British, and six to Chile as compensation for two dreadnoughts confiscated by the British. One British ship (H-41) damaged in a collision had been scrapped before commissioning, 10 ships

One of the H type submarines built at the Vickers shipyard in Montreal, 1916

were left unfinished. The construction of Holland's ships proved to be so good and robust that three navies still used them during World War Two. The last of them went for scrap after over 30 years of service. Perhaps the most interesting and dramatic events have been the part of ships flying the flag of St. Andrew, and then under the red banner of the "workers' and peasants'" fleet.

AG for "Amerikanskyi Golland"

The Russian fleet focused on the construction of large armoured warships, but from the beginning of World War One felt a painful shortage of submarines. The situation was tried to improve by directing orders for additional ships to local shipyards, but this proved to be insufficient. Shipyards overloaded with the implementation of previous orders had been slow to perform new tasks. In addition, the war had stopped the import of equipment and mechanisms coming from Germany, and elements made by the Allies were arriving with a long delay. The program of rapid strengthening of Russia's underwater force was a big question mark. In this situation, the only solution was to buy completed submarines overseas. Rescue came unexpectedly from across the ocean, from an old, proven submarine supplier to the Russian fleet - the American Electric Boat Company. On 22 June 1915, the Americans, through the "Noblesser" factory in Revel (today Tallinn, Estonia), offered the Russians three to five submarines of the Holland type, 355 tons surface displacement, built at that time for Britain, by the summer of next year. The price of each ship, depending on the quantity ordered, was set at 885-900 thousand US dollars. The ships were going to be built in Vancouver (Canada), and then delivered in sections by merchantmen to Vladivostok[1]. From there, by railway to Revel, where the "Noblesser" shipyard was to assemble them. Specialists from the Naval General Staff, having got acquainted with the technical documentation of ships and after consulting British colleagues who had already operated ships of this type, gave a positive opinion. The ships were to be used for combat operations in the entire Baltic Sea, and after the war they were used for training purposes. The only problem was the choice of the place of assembly of the ships delivered. It was feared that entrusting this task to the "Noblesser" shipyard would have a negative impact on the program of building the Bars class ships, which had been already delayed anyway. In this situation, the Navy Ministry announced a competition for the assembly of ships supplied from the States, which the Baltic Shipyard won. Such a solution was also accepted by the commander of the Baltic Fleet, Vice Admiral V.A. Kanin. Admiral Kanin even addressed the Chief of Staff, Vice Admiral A.I. Rusin with a request to move the "Noblesser" shipyard away from the assembly of purchased ships, because the shipyard could not comply with previously concluded orders. The Admiral's intention was also to free himself from the "monopoly of Lessner, Nobel and Bubnov family". The contract for the supply of the first five submarines, under the export name "602-F", was signed on 18 August 1915. It sought for an amount of 3,721,500 US dollars, i.e. $742,500 for each ship (7,239,375 roubles). An additional 1,340,250 roubles was to be the cost of ships' assembly in Russia. Delivery of the first three submarines was planned for April 1916, and the other two for May 1916.

From Vancouver do Petersburg

Ship sections, loaded on three transports ("Montigl", "Koan Maru" and "Gishen Maru") were delivered to Vladivostok. Only the first merchantman unexpectedly arrived at the Japanese port of Kobe. Hence the cargo was transported to Vladivostok by the Russian freighter "Tula". Supervision over the loading operation was carried out by engineer B.A. Lominitskyi, sent to America for this purpose. Checking of ships by rail from Vladivostok was managed by lieutenant M.V. Kopeyev (later lieutenant D.S. Karaburji). Both of them later supervised the assembly of ships at the Baltic Shipyard and then commanded AG type ships. The assembly of the sections began at the Baltic Shipyard on 2 April 1916. On 8 June this year, all five submarines officially found themselves on the fleet list. At the request of Vice Admiral V.A. Kanin they were given a letter-digit designation: "AG-11", "AG-12", "AG-13", "AG-14" and "AG-15". The letters AG were an abbreviation of "Amerikanskyi Golland". The assembly was supervised by a group of American specialists from the Electric Boat Company, headed by engineer E. Willar. During the assembly work a lot of minor flaws were revealed. The Americans did not carry out pre-assembly and fitting of individual elements of the structure, many locating holes were not drilled. The defects were remedied on the spot. Launching of the hulls took place by means of a floating crane in August 1916. Sea trials were conducted in the area of Kronstadt, Bjorke and Revel, under the supervision of American engineers R. Gilmour and W.W. Foster. The "Noblesser" shipyard

dealt with the rectification of defects which occurred during the tests. After official acceptance by the navy, one 47 mm Hotchkiss gun was installed on each of the ships. The first of the Baltic submarines "AG-11" was commissioned on 2 September 1916, and on 6 September the banner was raised for the first time and the ship started her operations, occupied mainly with crew training and removal of defects. From 4 November 1916, there were at half-hour stand-by status in Revel. The next was "AG-12", which entered service 16 on September this year. However, for a dozen or so months the "Noblesser" shipyard corrected defects. The "AG-13"," AG-14" and "AG-15" entered service on 17 November 1916. All five submarines formed the 4th Squadron with the ship base "Oland" (ex-German transport "Irma") and stationed at the Gange base on Hangö Peninsula (today Finland).

Description of the construction

Architecture
The design of the mono-hull submarine of the "602-F" project was similar to the American ship "Seawolf" (in service since 1913). The rivetted rigid hull had a cross-section in a shape similar to a circle, and in the stern area the shape of an ellipse. Bow and stern ended with steel solid stems, the aft part of the hull resembling the shape of a fish tail. The hull connections were made with a frame space of

"H-1" submarine, the first of a series of 72 submarines, 1914

One of the AG type submarines on the slipway of the Baltic Shipyard

Table No. 1. Torpedo specifications

Type	Entering service	Calibre, mm	Length, m	Weight, kg	Weight of explosives, kg	Range and speed, km/kn
45-10/15	1915	450	5.2	665	100	1/38
						2/34
						3/29
						4/25
45-36N	1936	450	5.7	935	200	3/41
						6/32

Table No. 2. Gun specifications

Type	Hotchkiss	21-K
Calibre, mm	47	45
Barrel length, calibres	35	46
Elevation, degrees	60	85
Muzzle velocity, m/s	701	760
Range, m	4000	4500
Rate of fire, rounds/min.	12	25-30
Endurance, shots	-	3000
Weight, kg - round - charge	1.5 0.35	1.41 0.36

ing air pockets that facilitated abandoning ship by the crew. All hatches could be opened and closed from the command post. In the first compartment, torpedo tubes, spare torpedoes, torpedo and communication hatches, bow battery set and officer's cabins were located. In the lower part of the compartment, fuel tanks and some of the main ballast tanks were placed. The second compartment was occupied by the command post. The combat bridge located above it had a lower and upper hatch, which allowed it to be used as an airlock for the crew to abandon ship in an emergency. In the third compartment there was a second set of batteries, some of the main ballast tanks, air compressors and electric stations, above them - the crew's forecastle, galley, radio and a hatch of the conning tower's cover. The fourth compartment - engine room, accommodated diesel engines and electric motors, main pumps and compressors, under them fuel tanks and differential tank. The upper part of the hull was covered with a superstructure with deck plating, inside of which there were steering mechanisms, capstans for the anchors: underwater one of 864 kg and surface anchor of 367.8 kg, exhaust silencers, signal buoy. Stern horizontal rudders were placed behind the propellers, which increased their efficiency. Bow rudders could be folded.

Ballast system
The ballast system was more modern and more reliable than on Bars class submarines[3]. It com-

470 mm, angle bars and a box keel. Plating thickness ranged from 9.5 to 11.1 mm. Flat bulkheads with a thickness of 12 mm divided the hull into 4 watertight compartments[2]. All compartments with the exception of the second one were equipped with entrance hatches, which had elongated collars, in the case of flooding the compartments mak-

Table 3. Specifications of the AG type submarines in various periods of service

Submarine	Projekt 602F	"Politrabotnik"	"Kommunist"	"A-4"
Displacement, t	1917	1924	1931	1943
- normal	355.7	357.2	355.7	355.7
- underwater	467	467	435	434
Dimensions, m				
- length	45.8	45.8	45.8	45.8
- beam	4.81	4.8	4.81	4.81
- draft	3.8	3.8	3.8	-
Reserve floatation, %	22	22	22	22
Metacentric height				
- surface	0.17	-	0.17	0.17
- underwater	0.27	0.38	0.27	0.27
Armament:				
- torpedo (torpedoes)	4 x 450 mm (8)	4 x 450 mm (8)	4 x 450 mm (8)	4 x 450 mm (8)
- gun (rounds)	-	1 x 47 mm (110)	1 x 47 mm (110)	1 x 45 mm (300)
- machine guns	-	1 x 7.62 mm	1 x 7.62 mm	1 x 7.62 mm
Top speed, kn				
- surface	13	9.1	12	12.8
- underwater	10.8	6.5	6.5	8.5
Range, NM/kn				
- surface	2200/13	3000/5.5	-	2700/12.8
- underwater	25/10.5	-	26/6.5	100/2.5
Drive				
- diesels, HP	2 x 240	2 x 120	2 x 240	2 x 240
- electric motors, HP	2 x 160	2 x 160	2 x 160	2 x 240
- fuel reserve, t	16.5	202 x 120	16	16.5
- batteries	2 x 120		2 x 120	2 x 114
Depth, m				
- working	45.7	45.7	27	40
- max.	61	61	45.6	50
Autonomy, days	15	15	14	13
Endurance under water, hrs	24	10-12	16	48
Crew	37	30	31	32

prised of eight main ballast tanks arranged fore, aft and amidships inside the rigid hull. Such a solution made it possible to blow ballast with compressed air at a pressure of 7 kgs/cm2 at a depth of up to 51.8 m. High pressure compressed air (176 kgs/cm2, weight 700 kg) was stored in 84 steel cylinders. The water from the ballast tanks was discharged through the box keel, used on ships of this type for the main draining. Self-filling ballast tanks with a total capacity of 86.52 t (78.3 t when underwater), equipped with large scuttles and ventilation valves. Placing ballast tanks inside the rigid hull forced its diameter to increase, but it also accelerated the process of submersion. Two trim reservoirs: "compensatory" and "central" were calculated for the pressure corresponding to the immersion depth of 100 m. For balancing the main ballast, pumps were used: centripetal with a capacity of 7.64 m3/h and a piston with a capacity of 0.76 m3/h plus three auxiliary and two manual. An interesting technical novelty was the presence of a special automatic valve for blowing the tanks in case of immersion to a depth of over 50 m.

Drive
The ships' propulsion consisted of two 8-cylinder diesel engines with a capacity of 240 hp each, made by the "New London" company from Groton. Maximum surface speed - 13 knots at 375 rpm. On one shaft with engines, 2-stage compressors (176 kgs/cm2) were installed. The underwater speed was provided by two electric motors that could develop a top output of 310 hp within one hour (10.5 knot speed). The economic speed was 5 knots (at a nominal output of 160 hp). The ships were equipped with two 3-blade propellers with a diameter of 1.39 m. The ships had a pipe (on the bridge between the periscopes) for feeding the diesel with air in turbulent weather. The electric motors were powered by a battery pack consisting of two sets (120 elements) with a total capacity of 720 kWt/h. This was sufficient for 25 NM of uninterrupted underwater travel. The surface range with the fuel supply of 16.5 t and 1.98 t of oil was 1,750 NM at 13 knots and 2,400 NM at 11 knots. At the trials, the ships exceeded the specified parameters: the range at 13 knots reached 2,200 NM, and at 11 knots - 2,580 NM. The entire electrical system with all receivers was supplied with 120 V of electricity from a battery with a total capacity of 720,000 Wt/h. The areas containing batteries were equipped with manual pumps for pumping out the electrolyte.

Armament
In the fore part of the rigid hull there were four single torpedo tubes of 450 mm calibre placed in pairs, one above the other. In addition to the torpedoes placed in the tubes, four spare torpedoes could be taken. The use of this option was however associated with a deterioration of living conditions

of the crew, therefore, until November 1943 it was not applied. The Whithead Model 1910/15 torpedoes were used. Just before the war, the tubes were adapted to the new 45-36N type torpedoes. The construction of the torpedo tubes allowed firing of no more than two torpedoes in a salvo (one after the other) from the lower left and upper right tubes, and vice versa. Firing a torpedo was possible from a maximum depth of 20 m. Re-loading the torpedo tube from a rack took 3 hours and 20 minutes. The gun armament included one 47 mm/35 AA gun (Hotchkiss) with an elevation to 60°, rate of fire 12 rounds per minute and range up to 26 cables. The cartridges were hand-fed through the working hatch.

Observation, radio-technical and navigational devices
The ships were equipped with two periscopes, one of which was located in the command post and the

"AG-11" of the Baltic Fleet

Two submarines of the AG type at the side of the base ship "Petr Velikyi" (a former battleship)

A group of four AG ships at the broadside of the base ship in Revel (Tallinn)

other on the combat bridge. Both had the same diameter of 127 mm, but different heights: 6.4 m the former and 3.96 m the latter. A searchlight with a diameter of 25 or 30 cm was mounted on the bridge. Lights and signals were fitted on two masts with a height of 12.2 m. Radio communication was provided by a wireless transmitter with a power of 1kW and an MW receiver Model 1901 or Model 1916 of PPS type. The navigation equipment consisted of two magnetic compasses and a "Sperry" gyro-compass.

Crew

The crew of the ship in the service of the tsarist fleet numbered 37 men, including 3 officers. Officers' cabins were located in the torpedo compartment, where there were three folding berths. The remaining crew had their own sleeping quarters near the fore and aft battery sets (16 men were allowed to rest in hammocks at one time). At the beginning of their service in the Soviet Navy, the crew consisted of 30 men including 5 officers in peacetime and 36 men including 5 officers during war.

World War One

"AG-24" on the slipway of the shipyard in Nikolaev

The participation of "agheshkas", as the type was popularly called in Russian, in The Great War was brief and not very successful, and their final fate

was tragic. In the campaign of 1917, they did not have the opportunity to encounter enemy ships. Only "AG-11" sighted a convoy of 9 large merchantmen under the escort of Swedish torpedo ships in the Gulf of Bothnia. Since the ships were moving within the territorial waters of neutral Sweden, they could not be attacked. Lack of contact with the enemy did not save the squadron from suffering losses. On 8 June 1917, during an exercise dive in the Bay of Lium, the "AG-15" sank. The reason was the stern hatch in the third compartment (the galley area), left open by a cook. Quick rescue came from a nearby mine-layer "Il-men", she rescued the commander Lieutenant M.M. Maximovitch, boatswain and helmsman, the fourth crewman - a navigator who also got to the surface – perished because he could not swim. After an hour, divers arrived and found that the ship was at a depth of 27 metres. They also discovered the presence of submariners still alive in the first and fourth compartments. A part of the crew headed by the First Mate, Leutenant K. Matseyevitch, spent 10 hours in the flooded torpedo room[4]. First, after 3 hours under the water, a test torpedo was fired containing a letter begging for help for 11 survivors. Then, still with no assistance, they raised the pressure in the compartment and opened the hatches. The air bubble that was created threw six men onto the surface of the sea, of which five survived. The remaining 18 crew members of "AG-15" perished along with the ship. At 1000 hrs in the morning on 10 June the rescue ship "Volkhov" arrived on the scene of the disaster, and between 13 and 16 June lifted the unlucky ship onto the surface. After a short refurbishment "AG-15" again found herself in service. However, the losses did not stop there. In September 1917, "AG-14" did not return from a combat patrol. She was commanded by the Senior Lieutenant A.N. Essen (son of the former commander of the Baltic Fleet, Admiral N.O. Essen). On 18 September 1917, she put to sea to her fourth combat patrol. Return was scheduled for 23 September. Probably the ship sank after hitting a mine in the area of Liepaja. On 8 July 1917, "AG-13" received a new callsign "AG-16"[5]. The balance of the achievements of the "agheshkas" was therefore modest: "AG-11" performed five combat patrols, "AG-12" four and "AG-13" only three. The remaining four ships of the 4th Squadron were mothballed with their base ship at the Gange port (Hangö, Finland). 1918 was end of the history of the Baltic "agheshkas". On 3 April German troops landed near the base in the morning. Ice-capped waters of the Gulf of Finland and the lack of an icebreaker did not allow the evacuation of ships. To avoid them falling into the enemy's hands all four ("AG-11", "AG-12", "AG-15" and "AG-16") together with the base ship, were blown up by their own crews[6] This is how the Baltic epic of AG type submarines, or project 602-F, ended in an infamous way.

The "agheshkas" for the Black Sea

Relatively good combat capabilities and performance values of AG submarines prompted the Russian Naval Ministry headed by Admiral Grigorovitch to order another 12 vessels of this type. In a short space of time, three contracts were signed (19 September 1916, 25 October 1916, 8 February 1917) for a total of 28,872,000 roubles excluding assembly costs. The first six ships intended for the Black Sea Fleet were slightly modified by Holland himself, without compromising their characteristics, previously approved by the Russians. They belonged to type 602-GF and 602-L. They were divided into two groups of three ships, delivered in sections by the merchantmen "Unkai Maru", "Garold Dollar", "Hazel Dollar", "Strida" and "Arabien". For unloading them in Vladivostok and sending them to Nikolaev responsible were Captain 1st Rank P.K. Ivanov and Lieutenant N.N. Mamoxivitch. The next six ships were intended for the Baltic and North (Icy Ocean Flotilla) belonged to type 602-R. The three ships planned for the Baltic Fleet were to be named AG-16, AG-17 and AG-18. All six were to be ready to be collected in September, but the formalities with their delivery stretched over time. The complicated situation in Russia after the Bolshevik revolution was not conducive to the finalization of the contracts. Finally, on 29 November 1917, the Higher Maritime College cancelled the order. The completed ships went into US Navy service named H-4 to H-9.

From Vancouver to Nikolaev

The assembly of the Black Sea "six" was carried out at the Nikolayevsky branch of the Baltic Shipyard (later "Russud"). Three representatives of the American company watched over the course of assembly of the first three ships: chief engineer M. Johston, engineer-mech. R. Gilmour and engineer-electrician T. Greaves. On the Russian side, S.S. Shaposhnikov was responsible. According to the schedule, the transfer of the first three ships ("AG-21", "AG-22", "AG-23") was to take place in the summer, and the second batch ("AG-24", "AG-25", "AG-26") - in the autumn of 1917. The assembly of the first ship began on 28 March, the second – 30 March, the third - on 29 April 1917. On 21 August 1917, the first three ships were entered on the listing of the Black Sea Fleet. When in 1918 the first ship, "AG-21", was commissioned, the civil war in Russia had already lasted for good. During his time, Nikolayev passed many times from hand to hand. New problems arose for the shipbuilders and things were getting worse. In the middle of May 1919, the work on "AG-22" was slowly approaching its end. On 21 June, the ship's acceptance tests began, among others immersion to a depth of 20 m. On 16 July 1919, the ship entered service, but due to a change of crew, Nikolayev fell

"H-12" submarine

into the hands of the Whites when they occupied the town for the second time, and on 5 August 1919, she entered service with the Sea Force of Southern Russia. Technical readiness of the "AG-23" at this point reached 60%. Meanwhile, instead of another ship in service, the first was lost. In December 1918, "AG-21" was taken to Sevastopol by the intervening Allied forces. On 26 April 1919, the Anglo-French troops leaving Crimea sunk the ship on the outer roadstead of the port in Sevastopol. "AG-22", managed to go out on a combat patrol, but on 14 November of the following year she left the home waters along with General Wrangel's squadron and went to Bizerta. There, after several years of rusting away, in 1933 she was sent for scrap. The remaining four ships were completed only in the 1920s and entered service under the Soviet flag.

"AG-23" goes to war against the Whites

Having evacuated Nikolaev, the Whites left the unfinished „AG-23" and „AG-24" on the slipways, and in crates delivered from America there were parts of the next two submarines of this type not yet unpacked. „AG-23" soon would become the first Soviet submarine in the Black Sea. The Bolsheviks were keen on quickly introducing the ship into active service. On 1 June 1920, for the launching of „AG-23" on the recommendation of V.I. Lenin, an authorized representative of the Central Committee of the Party A.V. Lunacharskyi

Torpedo compartment of the American "H-5" submarine (would-be Russian AG-17?)

Crew of "AG-24" (No. 13) on deck

visited Nikolaev. Despite the presence of a dignified visitor, she only slid one-third the length of the slipway and stopped, so had to be launched with a floating crane. The next day, the ship's acceptance tests began at the mouth of the Southern Bug River. The tests were carried out on 7-28 August according to a shortened program (without measuring the speed and immersion to its working depth) with great difficulty. On 18 September 1920, the ship officially entered service and on 22 September the Soviet flag was raised on the ship, she got her new name „Comrade Trotsky AG-23". The Bolsheviks had a serious problem with completing the crew for her. The situation was improved by the transfer (they arrived on 17 September) of 72 seamen from crews of four submarines in the Caspian Sea. Eight of them received the assignment to „AG-23", others went to several submarines under construction. On 4-5 October 1920, „AG-23", having broken through the sea blockade of Wrangel's fleet, sailed from Nikolaev to Odessa, from where she was supposed to operate against the white and interventionists' navies. After she had received 12 torpedoes from the Baltic Sea fleet she began to sail out for combat patrols. The Bolsheviks attached great importance to the operations carried out by „AG-23". This is evidenced

by a personal report from the commander of the Southern Front, M.V. Frunze to V.I. Lenin on 12 November 1920, informing of the order issued to „AG-23" to go towards the Crimea. In that area (Sevastopol) on 13-18 November 1920 „AG-23" performed her first combat patrol under the command of A. A. Ikonnikov. The arrival of the Soviet submarine in the Black Sea met with a reaction from His Majesty's government. In a note to the Soviet government on 26 September, the British announced that in the event of encountering „AG-23" British ships would attack. Another note was sent by the British in October after the first patrol of the Soviet submarine. This time they warned of the inevitable attack on Soviet submarines also in the Baltic Sea[7]. With the beginning of the evacuation of Wrangel from Crimea "AG-23" was putting to sea to intercept ships in the area of Sevastopol. On 21 February 1921, she attacked without success a French torpedo ship off the coast of the Caucasus.

Under the banner of the "workers' and peasants" navy

With shortages of almost everything: mechanisms, devices, equipment, instruments and fuel, as well as qualified personnel, the completion of the construction of the remaining ships posed serious problems. On 29 February 1920, the well-known naval engineer-mechanic I.S. Slodatov (delegated from the Underwater Shipping Board) appeared in Nikolaev, then occupied by the Bolsheviks, whose task was to check the possibility of introducing submarines into service on the spot. At the request of V.I. Lenin, submariners who were fighting on land fronts at that time were supposed to be sent to Nikolaev and assist in construction of the new ships. Due to the lack of other options on the ships, only one Italian 5.1-metre periscope was installed in the central compartment. On the day of the launch of "AG-23" the keel was laid for the next ship, "AG-24", which was named "Comrade Lunatcharskyi". Launched on 2 April 1921, the ship entered service on 22 July 1921. On 31 December 1922, it was given a new name – "Kommunist" - and the Secretary General I.V. Stalin became an honorary crew member. In July 1920, Nikolaev's shipyard workers began assembling "AG-25". Launching took place on 5 April 1922, 20 days before the deadline. On 26 May 1922, she entered service, but under the name "PL-18" ("Podvodnaya Lodka" for "submarine"). On 23 October 1920, in the presence of party officials - among others the Commander-in-Chief of the Armed Forces S.S. Kamenev - the keel was laid in Nikolaev for the fourth ship of the series the "AG-26". Workers were busy on it 24 hours a day. Due to the lack of the original engines, which in 1917 went to the submarine mine layer "Krab", a renovated diesel with a capacity of 120 hp produced

"AG-25" (No. 14)

Table No. 4. Construction dates of the AG submarines of the Baltic Fleet					
Name	Date				
	Listed	Keel laid	Launched	Commissioned	Banner raised
"AG-11"	04.06.1916	02.04.1916	07.1916	09.09.1916**	06.09.1916
"AG-12"	04.06.1916*	02.04.1916	19.08.1916	09.09.1916**	-
"AG-13"	04.06.1916	02.04.1916	31.08.1916	17.11.1916	11.10.1916
"AG-14"	04.06.1916	02.04.1916	09.1916	17.11.1916	19.10.1916
"AG-15"	04.06.1916	02.04.1916	09.1916	17.11.1916	30.10.1916

* According to other data 08.06.1916
** According to other data 02.09.1916

by the company "New London" was installed. The engines had been found in unusual circumstances: one in the laboratory of the Petrograd Institute of Technology, and the other on a ship based at the Volga Flotilla's base, "Martyn"[8]. Of course, this had a negative effect on the top speed of the ship. In addition, both engines worked clockwise which made it difficult to manoeuvre and maintain depth, but the shipyard workers did not want to change it for anything. On 11 July 1923, she entered the service as the last in the series.

In 1926, during training at the Diving School in the area of Sevastopol, a team of EPRON trainees found the wreck of "AG-21"[9]. Inspection showed the ship lying at a depth of 50 metres with a list of about 40° to the starboard side, the wreck was in good condition. However, lifting it proved to be a very complicated operation. Several attempts were unsuccessful, then work was stopped due to stormy weather. It was not until 21 May 1928 that the ship finally appeared on the surface. The hull of "AG-21", despite a few years' stay under water, turned out to be in better condition than ships currently in operation, because their elements had stood at the shipyard in the open air, which accelerated the process of metal oxidation. The ship's repair was made by the shipyard in Sevastopol, which had never done such works before. The renovation was completed and on 3 February 1931, the ship was already in the service again under a new name - "Metallist" (the new name was given on 15 October 1928). During tests on 19 December 1930, "AG-21" developed a maximum speed of 12.8 knots at 375 rpm.

The 1920s, the 1930s...

Maintenance of the AG ships originating from foreign purchases caused serious problems. First of

Table No. 5. Dates and results of the AG submarines speed tests		
Name	Period	Speed reached, kn
"AG-11"	24.08-2.09.1916	13.04/10,65
"AG-12"	7-15.09.1916	13,05/●
"AG-13"	24.09-17.11.1916	●/10,52
"AG-14"	4.10-17.11.1916	12,5/10,5
"AG-15"	14.10-14.11.1916	●/10,75

all, there were no spare parts, in particular battery cells and periscopes, which were not produced at home. In 1924, 9 million roubles were allocated for the purchase of essential equipment for the fleet. Later, this amount significantly shrank. At the end of the 1920s, the ships were approached their age limit and required a major overhaul. Regular dockings and repairs made it possible that the ships could be submerged to a depth of 40 metres. In early 1929, the general officer commanding of the Black Sea Forces launched a special commission to assess the condition of ships' hulls and mechanisms. Serious problems were caused by the diesel engines. In the absence of documentation, which was lost during the Civil War, the

Table No. 6. Construction dates of the AG submarines in the Black Sea					
Name	Date				
	Listed	Assembly started or keel laid	Laid	Commissioned	Banner raised
"AG-21"	21.08.1917	28.02.1917	19.12.1917	1918/03.02.1931*	-
"AG-22"	21.08.1917	30.03.1917	13.03.1918	16.07.1919	-
"AG-23"	21.08.1917	29.04.1917	01.06.1920	18.09.1920	22.09.1920
"AG-24"	-	22.11.1919 (again on 01.06.1920)	02.04.1921	22.07.1921	16.07.1921
"AG-25"	-	22.11.1919	05.04.1922	26.05.1922	-
"AG-26"	-	23.10.1920	24.02.1923	11.07.1923	04.07.1923

* Some references state 1918, but according to M. Morozov, „AG-21" spent the entire 1918 in Sevastopol (she did not have a battery) and was not put into service, and then sunk.

"AG-26" submarine (No. 15)

first four hydrogen combustion devices. The implementation of these devices took place up until the mid-1930s. Continuous changes were made to the ship's construction. The introduction of, for example, thermal insulation caused an increase in the weight of each ship by 640 kg.

Due to the favourable hydrometeorological conditions (all-year-round operations), the Black Sea was the right place to conduct a variety of experiments. Ships of the AG type for many years were the only submarines in this basin, so it is not surprising that they were chosen as guinea-pigs. One of such tasks was to test the immersion stability of a submarine remaining immobile under the water. The documentation obtained by the Soviet intelligence service in Italy in 1927 was used by "Ostekhburo" and engineers Bazylevskyi and Rudnitskyi to develop a home-made stabilizer. It was tested on "PL No. 12" ("Shakhtor") in 1931 and in 1933 on "PL No. 16" ("Metallist"). Despite the use of readily available documentation, the Soviets were unable to build a stabilizer. Much better results were achieved during tests of the dynamo-jet gun system so-called KPK ("Korabelnaya Pushka Kurtchevskogo" - "Kurtchevski's Naval Gun"). For this experiment, submarine "No. 14" ("Marxist") was selected. In 1932, the gun successfully passed tests on this ship. In the conclusion of the report, the commission stated that the 76.2 mm Kurtchevskyi gun with a set of 110 cartridges, could be installed in place of the 47-mm time gun and serve to combat surface targets, and on a special 90 cm high barbette also to fire at aircraft. At the beginning of 1934, 150 such guns were ordered. Five of them were to be mounted on the AG type ships. Then, it was even planned to install two guns on each ship[10]. Finally, Kurtchevski's guns were not installed due to insufficient tactical parameters and remained only a technical curiosity. In 1935, on "A-3" a new type of device for cutting anti-submarines nets was tested, and in 1936 on "A-1" the first model of Soviet hydrolocator was fitted. It should be noted that none of the tested devices or weapons were implemented in mass production.

The successful programme to complete the AG type ships did not mean the end of problems. Now new problems arose related to their everyday operations. About 70% of sailors serving on these ships did not have underwater experience. The result of this situation was frequent accidents and failures. And so, on 3 April 1930, at 0219 hrs the "Shakhari" (formerly "AG-23"), returning from a voyage, due to a navigator's fault, collided with a steamer "Elbrus". The cover of the right torpedo launcher, the bow stem, and the rudder was stuck. With the help of the steamer, the destroyer "Nepamozhnyji" and a tugboat, the ship was towed to base the same day. During the towing, the "Shakhtor" repeatedly hit the destroyer's broadside, ripping its plating with her rudder. On

Submarines "AG-24" and "AG-25"

Submarine "Kommunist" (ex "AG-24") late 1920s. In the foreground the gunboat "Krasnaya Gruzya" can be seen

regulation of the engines took place "more or less". The result was a difference in the specifications of each of the ships' engines. More importantly, the ships did not reach full speed, and the engines were overheating and damaged the piston cylinders. This defect particularly troubled the crew of "AG-26" ("PL No. 15"), on which, in 1924-1925, engines were only able to reach 240 hp. The batteries were "patched" by collecting individual elements from various ships of the tsarist fleet. Such a heterogenous collection was difficult to operate, and worse, deadly chlorine escaped from the batteries. It was not until 26 December that the Baltic Shipyard announced plans to produce the

the 8 June 1931, "Metallist" (formerly "AG-21") due to improper conduct of its skipper Bebeshin, was rammed during torpedo exercises by the destroyer "Frunze" and for the second time in her career rested on the bottom. A few men were on the surface of the water. A lifeboat lifted six, but not the commander of the ship, who drowned at once. On the sunken ship there were still 24 men who gathered in the fourth compartment and were waiting for help. Six hours after the catastrophe air was supplied to the ship. After two days, the ship, lying at a depth of 32 metres, was lifted by four floating cranes. Only nine crew members were saved, more than 20 died. On 1 January 1932 "Metallist" was in the line again. On 15 September 1934, her name was changed to "A-5".

Just before the outbreak of World War Two, all AG submarines underwent major repairs combined with modernization. The changes were not revolutionary: a rigid shield was placed on the bridge, the surface anchor was abandoned, and the 47-mm gun was replaced with a 45-mm 21-K semi-automatic piece with a reserve of 200 rounds. US-made electric motors were replaced with the Soviet PGB type. In the mid-1930s, an autonomous air regeneration system was developed by S.A. Bazylevskyi. Due to this, the ship could remain under the water for 48 hours. Also, some of the navigational equipment was replaced with elements produced in the USSR. Some of the ships received "Mars-8" noise-position-finders. Newer radio communication devices were installed: VHF "Mirage" and "B4-M2" sets, later replaced with "Buchta", "Dozor" and "Kub-4M".

Organizational confusion

From June 1939, all these ships were part of the 24th Squadron of the 2nd Submarine Brigade, commanded by Captain 3rd Rank A.S. Kudelia, and from October - Captain-Lieutenant G.E. Bobrov. After one year, "A-5" left and was delegated to the Training Squadron of the Underwater Detachment of the Black Sea Fleet. In February 1941, there was a significant reorganization of the submarine force, but in the case of the AG ships only the number of the squadron was changed to 6th. This situation lasted until August 12, 1942, when two brigades were combined into one. In the new structure, the "agheshkas" were included in the 3rd Squadron together with the ShCh V type submarines. At the same time a few months earlier - on 2 May 1942 - there was a change in the position of the commander of the squadron - the new one was R.R. Bump. This solution turned out to be unfortunate because both types of ships were very different in terms of tactical and technical capabilities. Therefore, already on 22 November the "agheshkas" were transferred to the 4th Squadron where M type ("Malyutka") submarines were used – of VI and VI-bis series. The squadron was

"AG-23" of the Black Sea Fleet

commanded by Captain 3rd Rank ŁP. Hijainen, and from 26 January 1943 - Captain 2nd Rank N.F. Klynin, and from 25 November 1943 – Capitain 2nd Rank V.S. Azarov. Another change in organization of the submarine force took place on 9 June 1944 in connection with the transfer of a large number of small M type ships to the Black Sea from the North and the Far East. Two brigades were re-formed. As part of the 1st Brigade, in the 2nd Squadron the AG type found themselves together with the "Shchuka" submarines[11].

World War Two

Contrary to the opinion issued in 1929 on type AGs by the commission for the inspection of all submarines: "The type AG operating in the Black Sea must be regarded as obsolete due to their construction and must not be considered combat ready for full scale war". Nevertheless, these ships were still operational and sometimes with good results. All the Black Sea "agheshkas" participated in World War Two. The beginning of Operation "Barbarossa" found them in Sevastopol with the 6th Squadron of the 2nd Submarine Brigade. From the main fleet base they operated in the first months of the war, then in November 1941 they

"AG-26" after returning from a training cruise, Sevastopol, 1930

Table No. 7. Dates and results of the AG submarines speed tests in the Black Sea		
Name	Period	Speed reached, kn
"AG-21"	-	•
"AG-22"	21.06-07.1919	•
"AG-23"	10-28.08.1920	11.34/•
"AG-24"	17.05-7.07.1921	12/•
"AG-25"	from 5.- 24.05.1922	•
"AG-26"	-	•

"A-5" submarine

the renovation was completed and the ship set off for a new base in Poti. By the way, the commander of the ship had for a long time served in the infantry and was transferred to the navy against his will. Having completed various types of courses, he was quickly promoted to the commander of the submarine. The real war for the "A-2" began only in the spring of 1942. On 7 April 1942, she came to Sevastopol for action against enemy shipping in the Odessa region. During the second patrol, she tried unsuccessfully to attack transports. On 27 May at 2235 hrs she was in Sevastopol at the wharf in readiness to put to sea, but suffered serious damage to the hull from close explosions of bombs during an air-raid. After partial repairs on 1 June she moved to Oetchmtchiri and from there to Poti for renovation. In the period from 7 May to 3 July 1942, she carried out several voyages to Sevastopol. In July, she sailed to besieged Sevastopol with a cargo of 11 tons of ammunition and 2.5 t of food, but shortly before reaching her destination, she was ordered to get rid of the cargo and hurry to Chersones to evacuate personnel. She returned to Novorossiysk with 11 artillerymen. On 4 August she was at a position near Odessa. As a result of improper manoeuvring, she lost the opportunity to sink a transport and suffered heavy damage. After that, the commander was brought to a martial court which sent him to the Marines. At the beginning of 1943 there were three patrols. In 1944 she did not participate in combat operations. She performed 21 combat patrols and one transport mission. She sank a large landing craft "F-474" (10 October 1943). After the war, during exercises, due to a navigation error, she hooked on the net barrier and suffered serious damage. After six months of renovation, she returned to the line of the fleet. On 12 January 1949, she was reclassified as a small submarine. It was not until 28 November 1950, after 29 years of service, she found her way to a scrapyard.

"A-3". On 22 June 1941, commanded by Senior Lieutenant N.I. Malyshev was undergoing renovation in Sevastopol, after a collision with a minesweeper. On 24 June, the renovation was completed and on 1-3 July 1941, the ship went

were ferried to the coast of the Caucasus to the port of Otchamtchiri. From the summer of 1942, they started operating against the enemy's lines of communication, mostly in the vicinity of bases and ports, most often it was the Odessa region. Here are the results of the actions of the ships and their final fate.

"A-1". On 22 June 1941, the ship was under the command of Senior Lieutenant S.A. Tsurikov and was undergoing overhaul in Sevastopol. Soon the renovation was suspended and the ship was mothballed due to the lack of electric motors, which were sent for refurbishment to Kharkov. On 3 November, Captain-Lieutenant B. S. Buyanskyi became skipper. On 26 June 1942 she was blown up because of the impossibility of going out to sea. At the beginning of 1945 she was lifted from the bottom and on 24 April 1945, removed from the fleet listing due to scrapping.

"A-2". On 22 June 1941, commanded by Captain-Lieutenant K.I. Chebyshev was undergoing a major refurbishment in Sevastopol. On 15 August,

Table No. 8. Dates and name changes of the AG submarines						
Original name	Changes					
	1920	1.10.1921	31.12.22	1923	3.02.1931	15.09.1934
"AG-21"	-	-	-	-	"Metallist" (No. 16)	"A-5"
"AG-22"	-	-	-	-	-	-
"AG-23"	"AG-23 Comrade Trotsky" (01.06.)	"PL-16"	"Niezamozhnyi"	"Shakhtor" (No. 12) 12.06.	-	"A-1"
"AG-24"	"AG-24 Comrade Lunatcharskyi" (01.06)	"PL-17"	"Kommunist" (No. 13)	-	-	"A-2"
"AG-25"	-	"PL-18"	-	"Marxist"(No. 14) 23.03.	-	"A-3"
"AG-26"	"AG-26 Comrade Kamenev" (23.10)	"PL-19"	-	"Politrabotnik" (No. 15) 23.03.	-	"A-4"

to Poti joining the rest of the squadron. On 11 November, Senior Leutenant Tsurikov became the skipper. On 24 March, during a voyage to Sevastopol, on the traverse of Krugloy Bay she was bombarded by ground-based artillery, dived and entered Sevastopol at periscope depth. She won her first victory during the next patrol (25.05 - 6.06.1942). On the morning of 29 May 1942, "A-3" under the command of Tsurikov, at a distance of 5 miles from Odessa, sighted a convoy of two merchantmen and seven cutters. Ignoring the limited depth, she penetrated the convoy and from a distance of 3.5 cables fired two torpedoes. One of them hit the second vessel in the formation which was the Romanian transport "Sulina" (3,495 BRT) going from Constanta with a load of coal and wheat. After half an hour, the ship sank to a depth of 24 metres six miles from Odessa. On 8 July, during a passage to the Odessa region, 25 miles to the south-west of Balaklava, she was strafed by a plane. During her 20th, and as it would turn out, the last patrol, the ship set off on 22 October. On 28 October "A-3" for the last time contacted command. She disappeared without trace, probably hitting a mine.

"A-4". 22 September 1941 found the ship in Poti under the command of Captain-Lieutenant A.P. Kasatkin. Already on the evening of 23 June she commenced the first patrol. In the second half of June she performed three transport missions to Sevastopol. Altogether, she completed 12 combat patrols and three transport missions. She was the only one of the "agheshkas" which was not successful in combat. On 22 November 1947, she was disarmed and removed from the fleet listing, and on 6 March 1947, was sold for scrap.

"A-5". On 22 June 1941, she was undergoing renovation in Sevastopol. On 27 June command was taken by Senior Lieutenant G.A. Kukuy. On 27 July refurbishment was completed and on 2 August "A-5" joined her sister ships in Poti. On 25 February 1942, she left Otchamcziri to Sevastopol for further raiding in the area of Odessa, but she only performed one patrol and on 27 March returned to the Caucasus. On 7 June she left Tuapse to operate in the Odessa region. On 11 June 1942, the ship operated in the area of the Odessa Bank, and sighted three transport vessels departing from the mouth of the Dnieper, accompanied by three tugboats and five sea-going self-propelled ferries as well as five mine sweeping cutters. A torpedo fired from the distance of 3.5 cables hit the Romanian merchantman "Ardeal" (5,695 BRT) steaming heavily ballasted, which suffered damage and was forced to run aground. The escorts dropped depth charges. Explosions threw up the ship, which then hit the bottom. The ship laid on the bottom at a depth of 18 metres. Once the damage was repaired, she left the danger area. On 25 July at 1108 hrs, also in the Odessa region, while underwater she hit an anchored contact

mine, which severely damaged the hull. The commander put the ship onto the bottom. At night at 2238 hrs, he surfaced and departed a few miles from this dangerous place. Enemy planes forced the commander to dive again. On 26 July having surfaced again, damage repair started. The fight to save the ship lasted four days, during which time the supply of food and fresh water ran out. Having partially coped with the damage, the ship began the return trip to base, where she arrived on 4 August and was refurbished for 22 months. On 15 May 1944, on the approaches to Poti, she was mistakenly attacked by a Soviet Pe-2 bomber, which dropped two bombs, but luckily they missed. She completed a total of 14 combat patrols. For the combat merits of "A-5" as the only ship among all this type, on 6 March 1945, she was awarded the Order of Red Banner. On 27 August 1945, she was withdrawn from the line, disarmed and converted into a floating battery charging station. In the mid-fifties, she was removed from the fleet listing and broken up for scrap.

Evaluation

Generally speaking, submarines of the AG type turned out to be ships featuring high reliability of mechanisms, good naval prowess, liveliness and a large number of rescue means for the crew in emergency situations. Some ships were active for about 30 years, they conducted combat operations during World War Two, even scoring victories. They can be safely included among the best submarines of World War One. In the 1920s they belonged among the best submarines in the Soviet Navy. Until the mid-1930s, they were included in medium-sized ships class, then they occupied a niche between small and medium submarines of the fleet. Even when compared to the small submarines designed in the 1920s, the "Malyutka" type, they looked quite good, not giving up their autonomy and surpassing them in torpedo equipment. Thanks to the successful arrangement of eight main

"A-3" submarine on the move

ballast tanks and the effectiveness of the stern rudders, the submarines quickly dived under the water, and were well controlled in the vertical plane going down to a depth of 50 m. Thanks to the streamlined shape of the hull, the loss of power was lower than on similar submarines of other projects. It is not surprising that the date of their decommissioning had been constantly shifted over time. They ended the war as the oldest combat submarines, in addition, some of them being successful.

SOURCE OF PHOTOGRAPHS: WUERTTEMBERGISCHEN LANDESBIBLIOTHEK, STUTTGART.

Bibliography

J.V. Apalkov, Bojevyje korabli russkogo fłota 8.1914 - 10.1917 g. Spravotchnik. St. Petersburg 1996.

V.V. Baabin, Podvodnyye lodki zarubiezhnykh proyektov v otetchestvennom fłote. Moscow 2008

S.S. Berezhnoy, Korabla i suda VMF SSSR 1928-1945. Spravotchnik. Moscow 1988.

P. Bozhenko, Krasnoznamennaya A-5. „Modelist-Konstruktor" Issue No. 7/1989

CKBMT „Rubin", Russkye podwodnyye lodki. Istorya sozdanya i ispolzovanya 1834-1923, Volume I, Part. 2. St. Petersburg 1994.

V.I. Dmitryev, Atakuyut podvodniki. Moscow 1973.

V.I. Dmitryev, Sovetskoye povodnoye korablestroyenye. Moscow 1990.

J. Flack, 100 Years of Royal Navy Submarines. Shrewsbury 2002

E. Ignatev, Podwodnye lodki tipa AG, "Modelist-Konstruktor" Issue No. 7/1989

E.A. Kovalev, Koroli podplava w more tchervonnykh valetov. Moscow 2006

L.A. Kuznetsov, Podwodnye lodki tipa „AG". „Sudostroyenye" Issue No. 7/1991

V.N. Maslennikov, Podwodnye lodki na Tchernom More w 20-oye gody. „Sudostroyenye" Issie No. 7/1986

M. Morozov, „Inostranki" Krasnogo Fłota. Moscow 2014.

A.V. Platonov, Entsiklopedya sovetskikh podwodnykh lodok. 1941-1945. Moscow - St. Petersburg 2004

Edited by V.M. Pashin, Otetchestvennye podwodnye lodki. Proyektovanye i stroitelstvo. St. Petersburg 2004.

Edited by I.D. Spasskyi, Istorya otetchestvennogo sudostroyenya. Vol. III St. Petersburg 1996

Sudovoy spravotchnik morskikh sil Soyuza SSR na 1924 god. Leningrad 1925.

"Warship International" Issue No. 3/1977

Collective, Boyewaya letopis VMF 1917-1941. Moscow 1993.

Endnotes

1. In accordance with international law, no neutral state could build ships for belligerents. To circumvent this, the Americans decided to prepare diesel engines, electric motors, batteries, etc., i.e. virtually the entire components of the ship, and assemble them in Canada.
2. During the overhauls in the 1930s, the first compartment was partitioned by a light bulkhead into two, and from now on the ship had five compartments.
3. „Bars's" - the colloquial term for „Bars" submarines designed by the well-known constructor I.G. Bubnov and built in large quantities in 1913-1917.
4. Konstanty Matyjewicz-Maciejewicz was a Pole and later served with the Polish merchant navy on the training sailing ships „Lwów" and „Dar Pomorza", he lectured at maritime schools in Tczew, Gdynia and Szczecin. Called "Captain of Captains", he died in 1972 in Szczecin.
5. „Warship International" provides information that the change of the number occurred after the ship sank and was later lifted.
6. One of these ships, „AG-16", was lifted in 1924 and placed on the strength of the Finnish Navy, but it was never repaired and was scrapped in 1929.
7. The reason for such a nervous reaction of Britain was the sinking of the destroyer „Vittoria" by a Soviet submarine on 31.08.1919. In retaliation in 1919, the British seized in Sevastopol and Odessa 13 submarines of the Black Sea Fleet and eventually sank them.
8. L.A. Kuznetsov, Podwodnyje lodki tipa „AG". „Sudostroyenye" Issue No. 7/1991, p. 56
9. EPRON (Expedition of Underwater Works of Special Importance) - an organization established to raise wrecks of ships and to carry out various types of underwater work.
10. There were also 152.4 mm DRP guns that were planned to be mounted behind the conning tower, one on each ship.
11. M. Morozov, „Inostranki" Krasnogo Flota. Moscow 2014, p. 37.

"AG-14" of the Baltic Fleet

An interesting photograph of the "Metallist" (ex "AG-21") during exercises accompanied by a floatplane, behind the conning tower the 47-mm Hotchkiss gun is visible

The Japanese Battleship

Ise

The Japanese Battleship Ise, 1944

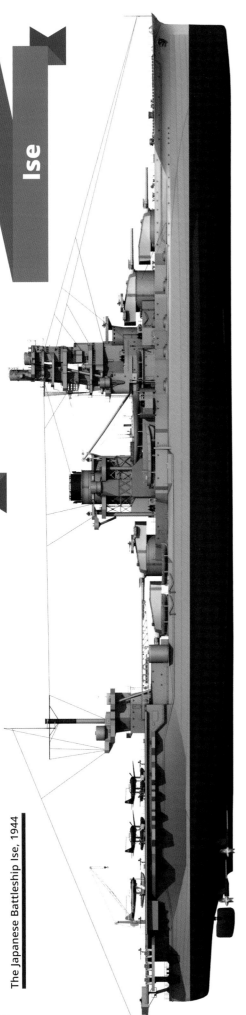

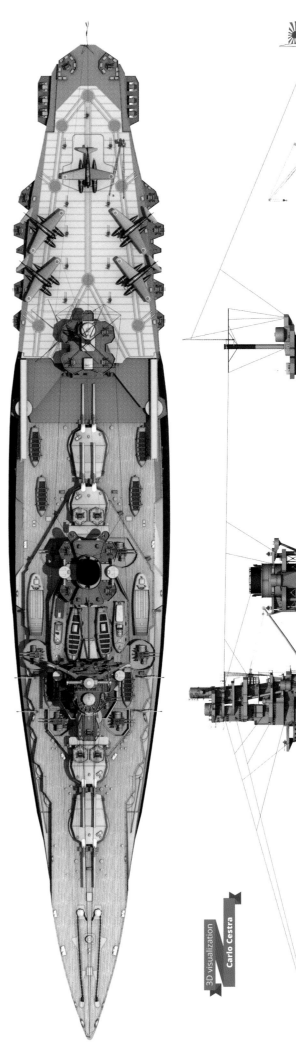

3D visualization

Carlo Cestra

The Greek Armoured Cruiser

Georgios Averof

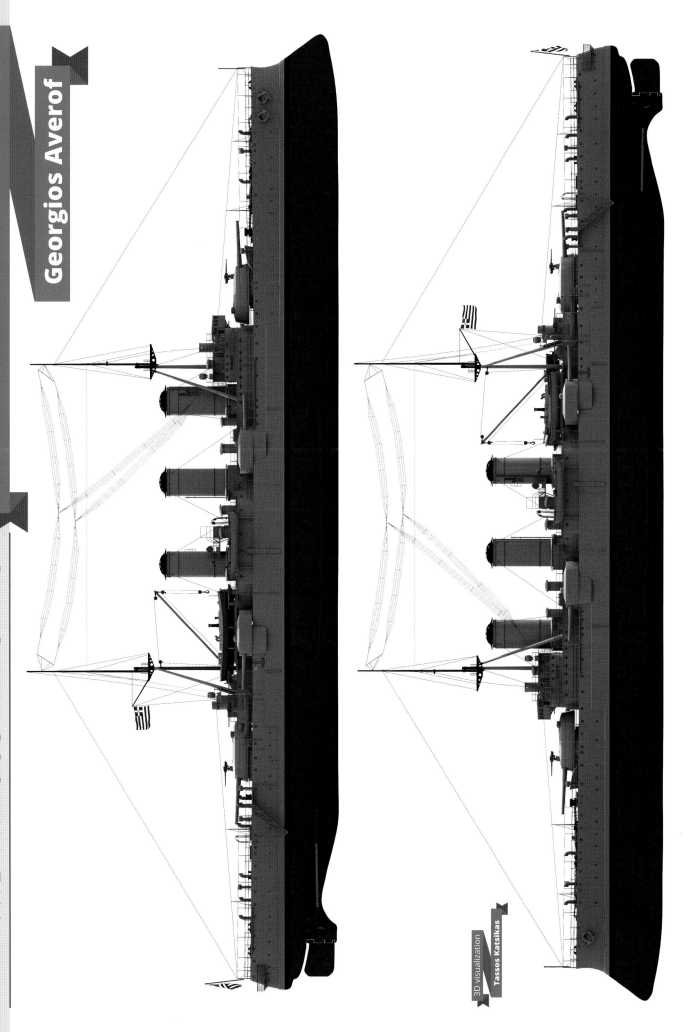

3D visualization
Tassos Katsikas

Gneisenau

Gneisenau at the beginning of 1941

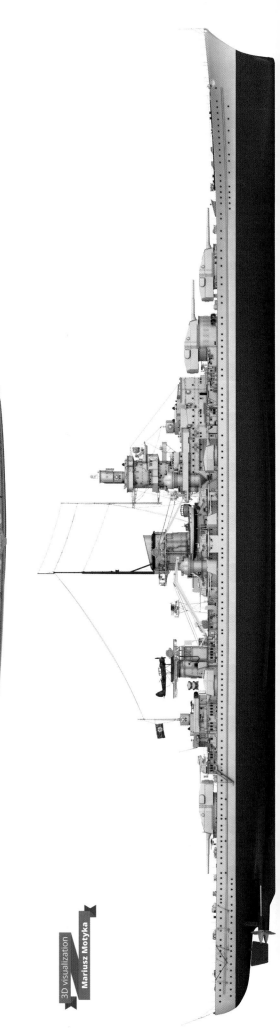

3D visualization

Mariusz Motyka

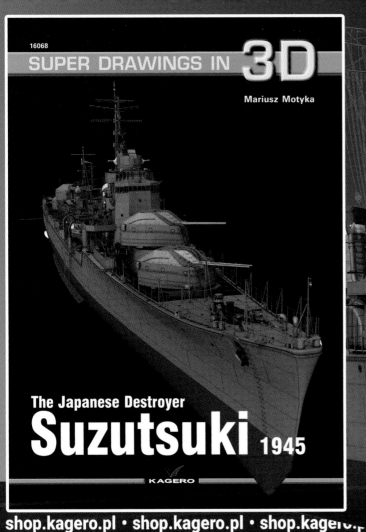

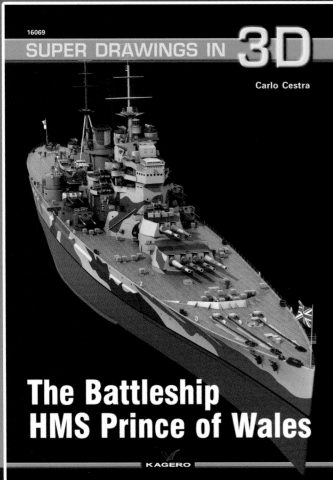

Italian Submarines In The Red Sea 1940-1941

Marek Sobski

„Galvani" submarine photographed from another ship during training in the Red Sea, April 1940 [„Storia Militare", No. 17]

The Italian presence in East Africa posed a threat to shipping coming out of the Suez Canal towards the south (the route connecting the Mediterranean Sea with the Indian Ocean). North and East Africa were important due to the possibility of blockading the land and sea routes to India, Malaya, Australia and New Zealand, and to the oil fields in Iraq and Iran, operated by British companies. Italian possessions in East Africa threatened Sudan (connecting Egypt with the rest of the British territories in Africa) and the dominance of Britain in the Red Sea.

Troublesome waters

To cut this sea route was attempted by the forces of the Italian fleet operating from the port of Massaua (Massava). The command of the Regia Marina in this part of the world was carried out by Marisupao (Comando Superiore di Marina in Africa Orientale Italiana – Naval Headquarters in Italian East Africa). Subordinated to Marisupao was also a group of submarines - Flottiglia sommergibili, composed of:

81. Squadriglia:
- "Guglielmotti",
- "Ferraris",
- "Galvani",
- "Galilei";

2. Squadriglia:
- "Perla",
- "Macallè",
- "Archimede",
- "Torricelli".

The Italian forces in East Africa fought their battles in conditions of total siege. It was necessary to calculate every mission at sea in terms of fuel consumption, oil, and torpedoes because they were items that could not be replenished. The Italian possessions, known as Africa Orientale

Italiana (A.O.I.), were supplied exclusively by an air bridge. Supplies for the army, air force and navy had to be delivered by air, and the shortages of basic military resources in A.O.I. were enormous. In addition, the air bridge was unreliable, running over hostile territory, and its northern flank was dependent on the changing course of the fate of the campaign in North Africa. Therefore, the focus was on transporting the most-needed material.

It is also worth mentioning the not-too-modern doctrine of the Italian submarine force, based on the experience of the World War One and its actions against the Austro-Hungarian fleet, which had absolutely nothing to do with the contemporary war against tonnage and shipping. The Italian submarines were assigned to strictly defined "hunting zones" they should stick to, or they were deployed near important enemy naval bases. The Italian commanders did not train for attacks on convoys; in peacetime they learned to approach a lone target, which was only occasionally accompanied by a ship pretending to be an escort; this of course also resulted from limited resources. In addition, it was ordered to engage enemy surface ships and aircraft on the surface.

For the first period of the war, a powerful blow was planned by the Italian Navy on enemy shipping in the Red Sea. The Regia Marina surface vessels in this area were obsolete, which is why the main attack force had to consist of submarines. In May 1940, it was planned to deploy them near all the most important enemy bases: Port

Sudan, Djibouti, Aden, Berbera and the Gulf of Oman. Such extensive action was not carried out, though – only scanty forces were available, losses were feared, and some operational ships and well-rested crews were to be kept in reserve.

The war began with deploying three submarines the area of Djibouti, Aden and Port Sudan. On one of them there was a breakdown and a replacement was immediately sent out to sea. Shortly thereafter, Prince Aosta demanded that two more ships should be sent to patrol the route between Djibouti and Aden and the roadstead of the former. These ships went out hunting during the southwestern monsoon. Submarines were the only modern ships of Italians in this area, but their efficiency left much to be desired. Activities in the Red Sea and Indian Ocean, the latter accessible through the Bab-el-Mandeb Strait, had their own specific demands.

Spring 1940, submarines and surface vessels Regia Marina in the port of Massaua [„Storia Militare Dossier", No. 12]

Italian submarines in the port of Massaua [Internet]

"Macallè" not long after launching in October 1936 [Internet]

"Macallè" before the outbreak of World War Two [Internet]

"Macallè" at the entrance to the port of Taranto ["Storia Militare Dossier", No. 11]

The region was characterized by very high air temperature (Massaua is one of the hottest inhabited places in the world) and very high humidity. The temperature inside the submarines could reach 45 degrees. The Italian submarines were therefore equipped with sophisticated air-conditioning systems with increased efficiency, working on methyl chloride (chloromethane). This odourless and colourless gas is highly toxic (also carcinogenic). A man forced to inhale it suffers severe poisoning, which in the mildest cases manifests itself with dizziness and numbness, further deterioration is possible, partial or complete loss of consciousness, lack of appetite, mood swings from euphoria to destruction mania, and even murder mania. The gas can also cause hallucinations, damage the nervous system, cause madness, and eventually lead to death. Problems with leaky air conditioning were diagnosed earlier, but joining the war so suddenly caused that this was one of many things that had not been dealt with, and the sum of such the issues led Italy to a catastrophe.

In the Mediterranean, everything worked practically without reservations, but the Tosi company's constructors in the case of colonial ships (such as the Brin and Archimede type) had to take into account the far worse conditions prevailing off the coast of East Africa. The weather made it

impossible to maintain the tightness of the air-conditioning system in the long term. In addition, leaks due to shocks from exploding depth charges had to be reckoned with.

Before the war it had been found that a possible gas leak was not a big threat to the human body. As a result of experiments carried out at plants producing air conditioning systems for ships, it was considered that only a high concentration of gas was toxic. However, this had nothing to do with the conditions onboard a submarine during a combat cruise, when heat, moisture, chlorine, carbon monoxide and other vapours could weaken a crew of 50-60 men in a closed environment in which it was difficult to provide adequate ventilation.

With the deterioration of the international situation, the training of Italian submariners was intensified. Between March and September 1938, there were four cases of crew poisoning, two of which occurred in the Red Sea. Earlier, in August 1937, the first such case in the Mediterranean occurred, when almost all of the crew of the submarine "Glauco" were poisoned. Between March 1938 and June 1940, there were as many as 20 cases of methyl chloride leaks in the Red Sea itself, another three occurred in the Mediterranean. In most of these cases, the crew did not suffer. Attempts were also made in the open ocean, eg in the spring of 1939 the submarines "Gemma" and "Perla" put to sea for a long experimental cruise in

the Indian Ocean during the north-eastern monsoon. There was dangerous gas poisoning on the ships, men lost their overall efficiency by inhaling dangerous fumes for less than a quarter of an hour. A report from this mission, dated 24 April 1939, very clearly highlighted the existence of such a threat.

From February 1938, *Comando Sommergibili* (submarine command) considered replacing this dangerous gas with freon, commonly used on US submarines, which had no toxic properties. However, it lacked the funds. Research was also commissioned to develop other alternatives, but Italy entered the war suddenly and the search did not bring any concrete results by that time.

Other problems also had to be tackled. Air humidity up to 100% caused large losses in electrical circuits and disrupted the operation of electric motors. When the south-west monsoon was blowing in the ocean, which was the strongest in summer especially (wind force 9), a submarine moved with difficulty. The pressure of the water on the bow made it practically impossible to maintain course. When under the water, it was almost impossible to use the periscope because of foam and splashes of water that "blinded" it. The waves made it difficult to maintain depth, which was hazardous as the ship could partially surface or disclose its periscope to the eyes of unwanted observers. All these factors became apparent in 1939 during an experimental cruise performed by

A 100 mm L/43 on the mount at the back of the "Brin" submarine conning tower. In the background cruisers "Bolzano" and "San Giorgio" are visible ["Storia Militare Dossier", No. 12]

the submarines "Otaria" and "Brin", which, moreover, encountered major problems using their guns in such conditions. Only the latter, thanks due to her gun being mounted on the conning tower, managed to open fire, but only when she was sailing at low speed.

The British and the French did not deploy their submarine in this region of the world, as Italian authors suggest - perhaps not without reason (unfavourable results of their own tests). The Italians undertook such a risk. The absence of British submarines in Aden or French ones in Djibouti is really surprising. The Bab-el-Mandeb Strait was poorly protected, the British believed that its shallow waters and shoals would prevent the passage of submarines. The Italians were passing it quite freely, and in 1941 they even managed to do the same with their surface vessels.

"Galilei" photographed probably in 1936 ["Storia Militare Dossier", No. 11]

A tanker "James Stove" (8,215 GRT), victim of "Galilei" ["Storia Militare Dossier", No. 12]

Madness under hatches

On 10 June 1940, around 4 pm, the submarine "Macallè" (tenente di vascello Alfredo Morone) left Massaua for a patrol in the area of Port Sudan. This port was founded by the British in 1909, it was at the end of the railway line connecting the coast with the Nile valley. "Macallè" was given the task of patrolling a 30 NM wide (or 22 NM) strip of water east of the coast. This entrusted task from the very beginning was risky, the last section of the route were waters dotted with tiny islets, reefs and shallows. The especially dangerous area was located south-east of the port. Having left its base, the ship soon dived into a deep immersion. Up to 0300 hrs navigation was carried out using the Cavet lighthouse, the last Italian one on the Eritrean coastline.

From 11 June heavy cloud persisted, which is why the navigational officer was unable to determine the position of the ship. There was no sign of clear skies. In peacetime, the route to Port Sudan was marked by lighthouses, which the British had built on uninhabited islands. Due to the prevailing conditions, the Masamarhu lighthouse was not identified, the southernmost of the three showing the way to the port.

Two days after putting to sea, one of the sailors belonging to the bow torpedo tubes' crew reported that he had completely lost his strength and was also losing consciousness. Suspicion fell on the damaged latrine, which had to be replaced by buckets, because it was attributed to the release of harmful fumes. Another reason could be excess of carbon dioxide in the compartments. Other cases of poisoning were soon reported. During the cruise, the sufferers were placed near an open hatch. The commander ordered giving milk to the crew.

On 13 June "Macallè" was already almost in its designated zone, the skies also cleared a bit, thanks to which it was possible to establish the estimated position of the ship. However, the situation under the hatches deteriorated, the navigational officer was ill, the condition of other patients worsened, and their number also increased. Morone also realized that his body did not react as it should. Work on setting the course became long and tiring. The compartments were ventilated, but there was no improvement. Some men were on the verge of madness.

On the morning of 14 June "Macallè" approached the coast. The sighted lighthouse was identified as located on the Sanganeb reef (it is at

"Galilei" leaves Taranto in the mid-1930s ["Storia Militare Dossier", No. 12]

its southern end, 16 NM north-east of Port Said). This was a huge mistake, in fact it was the Hindi Gider lighthouse, located on an island further south. It was a mistake of only 30 NM, but the ship was in waters extremely difficult to navigate. Morone ordered surfacing, but was not aware of his mistake.

In the meantime, it became clear that the crew was dealing with collective poisoning. Soon it was confirmed that there was a leak of methyl chloride. The installation was inspected after the first symptoms of poisoning, but no failure was discovered. The situation worsened constantly. Through a watertight door, open to the free flow of air, a naked man appeared, aimlessly wandering, apathetic with staring eyes. Others behaved in a similar way, raving something meaningless.

On the evening of 14 June Morone and his first mate decided that the mission should be aborted if care of the sick and fresh air flow did not improve the crew's situation. The only chance for the ship could be an immediate return to Mas-

sau. As it turned out, in the following hours the situation only got worse.

At the night of 14/15 June, at 0235 hrs, moving at a speed of 8 kn in waters full of rocks and shallows, at a course erroneously delineated by the navigational officer guasrdiamarina Elio Sandrami, "Macallè" ran aground straight on the edge of the sandy islet Barr Musa Kebir (or Barr Musa Chebir), approx. 65 NM from Port Sudan (approximate position 19°11' N and 38°10' E), the island itself of an area similar to a football pitch. Based on a previous observation of the lighthouse, Morone was convinced he was further north, in open waters. Now the ship was stuck with the bow raised and aft submerged, in hostile waters.

Part of the crew was evacuated ashore, attempting to bring the ship to deeper water. The ship had a very strong list to the port side. In the face of fruitless attempts, Morone decided to destroy the secret documents and evacuate the crew to the island, and all useful items were taken away. In the confusion or as a result of poisoning, another mistake was made: the code book was destroyed

"Galilei" on tow of the trawler "Moonstone", [Internet]

before the radiotelegraphist could send a coded signal. However, the use of the radio was doubtful due to the possibility of tracking the transmission by the enemy. After evacuating the crew and taking some of the food and water, the ship sank, falling down deep on the bottom at 400 m.

Morone consulted with his officers, it was decided to send a boat to Massaua (the Adua type submarines were equipped with wooden rowing jolly boats, hidden under light plating at the bow). The crew was to consist of three men. Sandroni got the opportunity to redeem his fault, accompanied by sergente Reginaldo Torchia and helmsman (nocchiere) Paolo Costagliola. They set off on 15 June at 2130 hrs. They were equipped with several packets of biscuits, a piece of smoked bacon, three bottles of water, a compass and a map of the Red Sea. They were the only hope for help for the rest of the crew. They tried to reach the Sudanese mainland (controlled by the enemy) at a distance of 170 km, and from there go to the border with Eritrea. At sea, each of the sailors had his own four-hour turn of rowing while another man was steering and the other was resting. There were no night breaks.

Meanwhile, the men remaining on the island found some wood, which had been thrown ashore by the sea, thanks to which they managed to erect a small hut to get some protection from the sun. They hunted for seagulls and crabs, eggs were collected. The distillation of seawater was also tried with little success.

On 18 June around 8 am, the three Italians landed on the Sudanese coast. Not far from the shoreline, the survivors stumbled upon a few hostile-looking natives, armed with scimitars. The Italians, however, were extremely thirsty, and un-

successfully tried to communicate, until Sandroni recalled the Arabic word for water. Finally, the Sudanese offered the sailors some dirty water. The Italians returned to the boat and sailed further to Eritrea. The next day they encountered an Arab boat, they learned from the crew that it was not far to the Eritrean coast.

The captured "Galilei" moored in Aden, 19 June 1940 ["Storia Militare", No. 17]

Late June 1940, "Galilei" at the British base in Aden ["Storia Militare Dossier", No. 12]

The anti-aircraft firing practice on an Italian submarine. The gunner fires the Breda Mod. 1931 cal. 13.2 mm twin-barrel machine gun ["Storia Militare Dossier", No. 11]

„Galileo Galilei" puts to sea from Taranto in 1935 [„Storia Militare Dossier", No. 12]

On the morning of 20 June the boat with the three exhausted Italians landed ashore. It seemed that they were lucky, as they came across Italian colonial soldiers who offered tea, camel milk and food. They had landed on Italian-held territory, but it was not the end of their odyssey, because the Askaris had no contact with headquarters. The sailors returned to the boat and went to Taclai. Along the way, they damaged their boat in the shallows, but they managed to patch it somehow. Once they arrived, they encountered an outpost manned by men of an infantry unit under lieutenant Currelli Curreli, who did not have the radio, but he immediately dispatched three of his men on camels to reach other posts and inform Massau. In five days the three survivors covered about 200 NM. Only now did the command learn of the "Macallè's" situation.

Soon, a Savoia-Marchetti S.81 bomber took off from Massaua, which on 22 June was spotted by a cook on the island. The plane dropped water, food, medicines and news about upcoming help. The submarine "Guglielmotti" immediately set off from Massaua. The British detected the stranded crew as well, their first plane appeared on 21 June. A note was dropped from it saying: "Write on the sand, what nationality you are and what state you are in. I will be back tomorrow." The Italians replied: *Italiani-Fame-Sete* (Italian-hunger-thirst). The next day, a message was dropped to the Italians, which informed them how the enemy envisioned their surrender. The offer included evacuation by par-

ties on a flying boat. On 22 June, around 1245 hrs, "Guglielmotti" showed up, but sottocapo silurist (torpedo mate) Carlo Acefalo did not live to see her – he died on 17 June due to heat and poisoning. The sailor was buried on the island. "Guglielmotti" had taken Dr. Origlia di Torino aboard to help the survivors. Some of the victims still suffered from the effects of poisoning and the hardships of being on the island, so that some of the way to Massauy they were tied up.

Guardiamarina Sandroni received the Medaglia d'Argento al Valor Militarei[1]. The hero of this story himself wrote down the symptoms of gas poisoning, which he observed: "loss of intellectual ability, continuous arguments, laughter without reason, sentences without logic, and even halluci-

nations (...) also poisoned was tenente di vascello Morone, who felt a sense of apathy and general exhaustion (...) some men of Macallè were completely naked, others wore their uniforms as if off duty"[2]. The skipper stood in front of the commission to explain the circumstances of the ship's loss, Morone was acquitted, and gas poisoning was considered as the main perpetrator of the disaster. Later he took over the command of the submarine "Asteria".

Massacre on the "Galilei"

On the morning of 16 June 1940, "Galileo Galilei" (capitano di corvetta Corrado Nardi), which six days earlier had put to sea and - undetected – passed through the Bab-el-Mandeb Strait and in

„Galvani" after launching in Taranto, 27 May 1938 [„Storia Militare Dossier", No. 12]

„Galvani" set sail in Taranto in the late 1930s [„Storia Militare Dossier", No. 12]

the Gulf of Aden sank the Norwegian motor tanker "James Stove" (8,215 GRT), built in 1931 by Caledon Shipbuilding & Engineering Co. in Dundee (until 1935 it was called "Bralanta"), carrying a cargo of 10,800 t of aircraft fuel. The ship was in British charter (by the "Shell" fuel company). On 29 May she left Singapore and headed towards Suez, she was to leave part of the load in Aden. 12 NM from the port from the tanker's deck a surfaced submarine was sighted, located at 4 NM on the starboard. The submarine moved on a parallel course and in the same direction. The submarine was not flying any flag, but the tanker's skipper assumed that it must be a British or French vessel.

Around 0515 hrs "James Stove" changed course, following the guidelines, into the mineswept channel south of the Elephant's Back lighthouse. "Galilei" then accelerated, taking a position slightly behind the stern of the ship, on the starboard. A signal lamp flashed from the bridge of the submarine: "stop your engine". The Norwegian ship stopped and identified herself. The Italians demanded sending a boat. A chief officer was sent on a mission from the tanker. When the boat came to the side of the submarine, Nardi informed them in a gentlemanly way that his ship

belonged to the Italian Regia Marina and in 25 minutes the tanker would be sent to the bottom because it was heading to a hostile port. At 0625 hrs, the tanker was hit by three torpedoes. "James Stove" sank at 12°35' N and 45°03' E. The entire 34-man crew was saved, the Italians had waited until the last man left the ship. A huge column of smoke rose into the sky. The Italian consul in Aden later confirmed that the smoke was visible from the mainland.

The trawler "Moonstone" (615 t, 102 mm gun, two Lewis 7.62 mm machine guns, two stern depth charge release rails for a total of 10 charges and ASDIC, skipper boatswain William J.H. Moorman) arrived at the scene of the incident, but did not find the attacker, she only towed lifeboats with survivors to Aden. The sinking of the tanker gave rise to an intense search action. "Galilei" was tracked by the destroyer "Kandahar" and the sloop "Shoreham". Air reconnaissance was conducted by a "Walrus" flying boat from the New Zealand light cruiser "Leander".

In the afternoon of 18 June, "Galilei" stopped the Yugoslav freighter "Drava". The merchantman was searched and released. However, a warning shot fired across the bow of a vessel was heard on

the British coastal outpost. The area around Aden was patrolled by a "Gladiator" (F/O Haywood) from 94 Sqn. RAF. At his request a "Blenheim" (or two) arrived from 8 Sqn. and a Vickers "Vincent" biplane. The Italians sighted these planes, but they did not dive (they could have done so right away, as soon as the Haywood's fighter was observed), and they decided to defend themselves on the surface. The duel took place around 1630 hrs. The "Blenheim" missed. The "Vincent" managed to drop two depth charges, but they were very inaccurate, so that it was almost thrown into the water by their explosions. Also the fire from the Italian Breda machine guns was inaccurate. Finally, the "Galilei" went underwater. The aforementioned hunting ships arrived after nightfall. The Italian submarine was also sought from the air the following day, they dealt with "Blenheims" of 203 Sqn. The Italians were not looking seeking escape, Nardi obviously did not want to leave the sector assigned to him.

At 1830 hrs, the *sommergibile* surfaced to charge batteries[3]. Finally, Nardi could see silhouettes in the darkness. The charging of the batteries was stopped and an attack was attempted, but the ship failed to take a suitable position before she was detected. The only thing left was to dive under the water.

An hour after surfacing, the Italian submarine was spotted from "Shoreham". The British went to the place where the submarine had disappeared, which was tracked with ASDIC and attacked twice. After the explosion of depth charges, contact was lost. It was not recovered, but "Moonstone" arrived in the meantime, which now independently took over the pursuit (the other ships returned to Aden). The area was also patrolled by "Blenheims" from 203 Sqn. However, these forces were quite modest, so much so that between midnight and 0230 hrs "Galilei" sailed undisturbed on the surface. The attack had however taken its toll on the Italian crew, already exhausted by terrible heat and rough seas. The air-conditioning system broke down, there were some cases of poisoning. The air below the deck was not cooled, it was heavy and damp.

On the morning of 19 June, the weather deteriorated, high waves were breaking over the deck. Nardi laid the ship on the bottom, 45 m under the water, all equipment was turned off, the crew had some rest, limiting their activity so as not to consume air and make no noise.

The trawler "Moonstone" was instructed to continue her search for "Galilei". Finally at 1137 hrs, at an approximate position of 12°48' N and 45°12' E, the ASDIC on the trawler made contact. In order to launch an attack, the British ship had to move against the waves, which greatly reduced her speed. Boatswain Moorman feared that dropping depth charges with fuses set for shallow explosion would damage his vessel, struggling with the seas, so it was decided to drop only one charge. It was dropped 14 minutes after contact had been established.

After the explosion, contact was lost, it seemed they missed. Soon the work of the hydrolocator resulted in finding the contact again, the underwater enemy was now near to "Moonstone". Immediately the trawler set a course to the place where two more depth charges were dropped with a six-minute interval.

Under the water, the Italians listened out with a hydrophone, it was considered that the enemy was a small vessel, it was accurately estimated that perhaps it was an armed trawler. Nardi or-

Duel of „Perla" with enemy ships immortalized on a postcard from 1940 [Internet]

Savoia-Marchetti S.81 from 14. Squadriglia, here in the hands of the opponent. The availability of bombs in East Africa was a big problem. 250 kg bombs were kept in reserve for raiding the ships detected in ports. Ships at sea were supposed to be attacked with bombs of only 50 kg of weight [Internet]

„Torricelli" in
Taranto, probably
summer 1939
[„Storia Militare
Dossier", No. 1]

Wreck of the
destroyer
„Khartoum" near
the island of Perim
[„Storia Militare
Dossier", No. 12]

dered to go to periscope depth, despite the view which was obscured by salt and splashes of water, he saw the pursuer and now was sure that his opponent must be poorly armed. After three minutes, "Galilei" surfaced, about a mile behind the stern of the enemy trawler, and the crew manned the guns and two 13.2 mm machine guns, which were taken out from under the deck. The Italian gunners, however, fired inaccurately. The gun's sighting system located at the bow was flooded with water, and it was most certainly damaged due to shocks from the exploding depth charges. An officer was correcting the fire with his binoculars, and the accuracy of the fire depended only on the gunner's eye. The rough sea and the blinding tropical sun made the whole thing even more complicated. The aft gun fared better, as it was somewhat shaded by the conning tower, but the monsoon conditions did not allow for effective fire.

"Moonstone" turned back and headed towards the "Galilei", wanting to reduce her profile and make it difficult for her opponents to aim. The British also opened fire from their gun, it was much more accurate than the Italian fire, two rounds, one after another, hit the bridge, each time killing and wounding Italian seamen. On the first hit, Nardi was wounded, and now with a bleeding shoulder he called on his men to keep calm and focus on firing. The third accurate round

caused further losses on the bridge, also killing the commander. Fire from various quadruple machine gun posts was also carried out, the bullets of which ominously ruffled the water near the Italian ship.

There was a massacre on board the Italian submarine. The commander, his deputy, tenente di vascello Bruno Ferraiolo and 13 other officers, non-commissioned officers and seamen died. Probably nine more Italians were wounded. The crew lost control of the situation, almost all non-commissioned officers were dead, only a young warrant officer (guardiamarina) sent with the reinforcements, who recently graduated from the accelerated course at the Naval Academy in Livorno (*Accademia Navale di Livorno*), but he also was wounded although at this point the task of commanding the ship would fall onto his shoulders.

The distance between enemies dropped to 450 m, the "Galilei's" deck began to be swept with a series of machine gun bullets, and even 7.62 mm rifles were fired. The Italian gunners suffered heavy losses. Someone stopped the engines. The sailors began coming out from under the deck through hatches, white flags were waved. The submarine stopped. At 1225 hrs firing ceased. Perhaps the Italian sailors were seriously poisoned with methyl chloride[4]. The ship was unable to submerge due to damage sustained in the duel with "Moonstone". The entire crew gathered on

the deck. Commanderless, the Italian sailors surrendered.

The trawler approached the capitulating "Galilei" and took survivors from her deck. Four men were wounded, one of them later died, so the clash caused a total of 16 Italians killed. The trawler skipper was afraid to send a boarding party onto the submarine, anxiously watching the large group of prisoners on board. Such an opportunity could have been lost forever, as a British plane appeared over "Galilei", fired at her and dropped two inaccurate bombs. At 1334 hrs, the destroyer "Kandahar" arrived on the scene, only now did a British boarding party enter the submarine. An attempt at towing was unsuccessful, the rope parted quickly. The British, however, started the "Galilei's" engines, and she reached Aden under her own power. She was sailing with a Royal Navy ensign flying above the flag of the Italian Navy. According to the British, the ship did not have any leaks and could move underwater, which contradicts the information given by Italian historians.

The enemy searched the submarine thoroughly, finding Italian codes and orders for ships operating in that area. This shameful omission can only by explained by the death of officers and the poisoning of the crew. "Torricelli's" and "Galvani's" crews would soon pay for this. All Italian ships that left Massau on 10 June were now exposed as if on a board, the opponent could easily establish the estimated position of each of them. Having returned from captivity, members of the crew of "Galilei" were interrogated, all unanimously and independently claimed that the secret documents were destroyed before the British came on board. Few of these men were anywhere near the command post and could witness the possible destruction of documents.

The Italian submarine, first as X.2 and later P 711 (from June 1942) served with the Royal Navy, initially as a power plant in Port Said, then a training ship in 1941-1944 (successively in India and the Mediterranean). In 1946, she was scrapped at Port Said.

The loss of "Galvani"

On 10 June at 0400 hrs "Luigi Galvani" (capitano di corvetta Renato Spano) left Massaua to take up

"Ferraris" in Messina in the thirties [„Storia Militare Dossier", No. 12]

Archimede type submarine, probably „Ferraris", in Taranto in the second half of the thirties [„Storia Militare Dossier", No. 12]

„Ferraris" in Naples in 1938 [„Storia Militare Dossier", No. 12]

a position in the waters of the Gulf of Oman. She was to attack tankers sailing from the Persian Gulf to the Indian Ocean. The mission was planned to last 28 days and only a few of them were to be spent in the operational area. The Italian ship easily reached the indicated sector late in the evening of 23 June, but it was greeted by emptiness. Thanks to the booty found on the "Galilei", the British already knew about the operation, tankers were sailing by a different route. Spano ordered to remain on the surface. A report from one of the Royal Navy officers: "The operational orders from Galilei state that Galvani left Massau on 10 June and that she should reach the Gulf of Oman, then operate within a radius of 8 NM from the entrance to the bay". Shipping was suspended, the corvette "Falmouth"[5] and the destroyer "Kimberly" arrived at their designated positions[6]. The trap was set.

By the way, it is worth correcting the information that on 23 June, the Indian patrol boat "Pathan" was sunk by "Galvani". Five crew members, including the skipper, were killed during the incident, but the Indian boat sank because of an accidental explosion of its depth charges. The "Pathan" was then in the Bombay area, and the Italians were only approaching the Gulf of Oman.

So in the evening of 23 June "Galvani" was sailing on the surface, the air conditioning system broke down, under the hatches there was merciless heat. In the meantime, enemy ships began combing the area. Two hours after midnight, "Galvani" was sighted from HMS "Falmouth" (Lt. Cdr. C. Hardy), about two and a half miles distant, visible only as a shadow. Soon it was clear that the shape observed was a submarine moving on the surface. At 0208 hrs, a request for identification was sent using Aldis. There was no response, so the 102 mm gun commenced firing.

A moment earlier the lookouts on "Galvani" saw 700-800 m in front of the bow, on the starboard, a large dark shape. It was the "Falmouth". The submarine was hit twice, first at the stern and then at the conning tower, which was pierced at the moment when the commander closed the bottom hatch above him. The Italians dived, but the submarine was descending under the water slowly, markedly bow down. At one point, "Galvani" sharply listed to one side, the keel of "Falmouth" caught on its stern which just a few seconds earlier had slid under the water. An attempt was made to correct the ship's orientation.

Immediately depth charges with their fuses set for shallow detonation fell on the Italians. The lights went out, and there were reports of damage: the rudder was jammed, the port side electric motor stopped, the output of the starboard one dropped, there was no communication with the extreme aft compartments. All pressure gauges in the command post were destroyed, and the instrument panel originally attached to the wall found itself in the middle of the room. Water began to break into the stern compartments, causing "Galvani" to quickly plunge stern down. The Italians did not deceive themselves that she could be saved, therefore the classified documents were destroyed.

Spano ordered to surface, but it would have proven impossible had 28-year-old petty officer – torpedo specialist (secondo capo silurista) Pietro Venuti, who was in the aft torpedo room, slammed the watertight door behind him to save the ship and her crew, sacrificing his own life. Thanks to him, 31 of the 57 crew members were saved. Venuti received the *Medaglia d'Oro al Valor Militare*[7] for this heroic act. There was already a lot of water in the hull, the damaged ship was surfacing with difficulty. "Galvani" emerged only partially.

There was nothing else to do but to issue the order to abandon ship. The gun was out of use, and the machine guns could not be taken out and put on their mounts. The crew began to leave the ship through the hatch in the conning tower. At this time Spano's deputy officer, sottotenente di vascello Mondiani, jumped through the hole in the conning tower caused by an explosion on the deck behind it, as he wanted to open the aft torpedo hatch to give the men in the stern a chance to escape. Unfortunately, before he got to it, the hatch disappeared under water, which in the meantime was already reaching the conning tower. The last men jumped off the deck when water was flooding the command post. After two minutes on the surface, the ship quickly began to sink stern down, taking 25 men with her. One of the sailors perished under the water once he abandoned ship. It was 24 June 0217 hrs. "Galvani" sank at 25°55' N and 56° 55' E.

No fire was opened at the sinking ship. The British quickly dropped their lifeboats onto the water. Spano and three officers were rescued. Almost the entire crew of stern compartments was lost. When hitting the submarine, "Falmouth" severely damaged her bow and spent two months under repair carried out in Bombay.

The explanation for awarding Venute with the decoration (born 10 June 1912 in Codroipo, Udine province) was as follows:

"While serving in the stern torpedo compartment of the submarine, which during a laborious naval mission in the seas distant from the motherland, was unexpectedly attacked under the water by the main opponent's forces, he distinguished himself by courage and bravery. The stern was damaged to an irreparable extent by a gun round opening a dangerous way in for the water into the room entrusted to him. Instead of seeking his own safety, being aware that he was condemning himself to certain death, he calmly locked the watertight door.

Thanks to his conscious and silent sacrifice, the entire submarine avoided sudden flooding, and it enabled survival for the majority of the crew, while he - who for the homeland and for the sense of duty sacrificed his life - disappeared into the sea together with the ship, which then went to the bottom.

A shining example of exalted military virtues (Arabian Sea, June 24, 1940)"[8].

The unusual cruise of "Perla"

In the afternoon of 19 June 1940, the submarine "Perla" (tenente di vascello Mario Pouchain) set sail for her first combat patrol. Her task was to hunt in the Gulf of Tadjoura, where the ship was to stay

"Archimede" in Bordeaux after her cruise from East Africa [„Storia Militare", No. 105]

"Guglielmotti" in Bordeaux, May 1941 ["Storia Militare Dossier", No. 12]

until 9 July. The mission was carried out at the request of the viceroy of Ethiopia, Prince Aosta. On the night of 19/20 June, the ship was moving on the surface on the safe route (*rotta di sicurezza*) in the southern channel of Massaua. At dawn, she went underwater and continued her journey immersed. Soon the air-conditioning system started to fail, the temperature inside the ship increased. At 11 am the first incident occurred, one of the electricians got heat stroke. Despite rubbing him regularly with ice, the sailor remained in poor physical condition until the end of the mission.

On 21 June the difficult decision was made to clean the filters, everybody was aware that some amount of poisonous gas would escape, but according to technical data it was assessed that

it would not be dangerous for the health of the crew. At night, men started working. The job was supposed to be simple and quick, it was carried out for greater security on the surface. The next day, five men showed symptoms of poisoning. The first mate, tenente di vascello Simoncini, demonstrated symptoms of mental disorder. The sick were placed in the bow torpedo tube room, the chief torpedo specialist took care of them, but the situation was getting worse, some men already had symptoms of total madness. Captain Pouchain decided to continue the mission.

On the night of 22 June the Bab-el-Mandeb Strait was passed. The "Perla" continued at full speed to reach her designated zone. At dawn, the ship laid on the bottom. There were scenes from horror movies under the hatches. One of the sailors was shouting, he was completely naked, but he wore two helmets on his head, and he wanted to go ashore. Another could almost have scuttled the ship, as he was fumbling at the valves. There were songs and vulgar cries. The men in better condition struggled with the sick who refused treatment. At sunset on 23 June the ship surfaced and continued her cruise, but nothing significant was observed. In the meantime, "Ferraris" came back to Massau, also with a poisoned crew, and news about the fate of "Macallè" were also received.

"Perla" was ordered to return to the base immediately, and at night she set a course to Massaua.

On 24 June, on the return course, half of the crew was already unfit for duty, several men had to be tied up. During the day, the ship laid on the bottom, the temperature inside reached 64° C. Under the deck it was terribly stuffy. Symptoms of sickness began to be demonstrated by the skipper and the chief mechanic. Pouchain was vomiting and dizzy, he was rapidly losing his strength, unable to command the ship in such a state. Navigation was performed with much improvisation, as was identification of the characteristic features on the coast. Somehow, she passed the Bab-el-Mandeb Strait undiscovered. This was done under water at dawn of 25 June. At sunset, the cruise was resumed on the surface.

On 26 June one of the sailors died, others could soon follow in his footsteps. The sick in the worst condition were given injections of camphor oil. It seemed that improvements were observed in some cases, but this was more the result of their self-suggestion. The commander, contacting the base in Massaua, gave his position in the area of the lighthouse Sciab Sciach (Shab Shak), he also asked it to be turned on to facilitate navigation. Switching on the lighthouse alerted the British or perhaps they intercepted the Italian signal.

"Ferraris" arrives at Betasom, on the platform there is a French pilot, who was responsible for the safe passage of the ship in the waters of the Gironde ["Storia Militare Dossier", No. 12]

Tenente di vascello Bruno Napp in front of the crew of „Perla" just moments before the visit of Admiral Angelo Perona, commander of the Atlantic grouping of Italian submarines [Internet]

„Archimede" at the Betasom base, May 1941 [„Storia Militare Dossier", No. 12]

Pouchain decided to surface before sunset and speed to Massaua full ahead. The commander felt bad, he could not move, he did not even go to the bridge. The post was taken by sottotenente di vascello Vinotti and guardiamarina Gallo, they searched for the shoreline with binoculars. This did not last long, the British sloop "Shoreham" was observed, steaming towards "Perla" at full speed. The enemy was 3,000 m behind the stern. The men on the platform did not wait for the command, they ordered diving on their own responsibility. Captain Pouchain, who felt a bit better, ran to the command post and was personally instructing his sick crew. The ship laid on the bottom at 24 m. The British began their attack with depth charges. They were exploding at different distances, some were close, fortunately there was no major damage. The enemy was circling over the submarine for several hours, but finally he sailed away. Initially, Pouchain moved towards the shore under the water, but he was afraid he would run aground.

As soon as it became possible, "Perla" surfaced again. 80% of the crew was poisoned to varying degrees. Strong currents meant that control over the position of the ship was lost. It was necessary to locate land or preferably the light of the Sciab Sciach lighthouse. Pouchain had probably sailed west for too long, the commander began to fear that he would be too close to the invisible shore, ordered a turn, and... the ship ran aground at Cap Ras Cosar, 20 NM south of Sciab Sciach. The exact time is not specified, but it was evening and most likely already a bit dark. Subsequent explanations before the specially appointed committee explain that some of the crew were unconscious and many were not fully conscious, including the skipper. They managed to contact Massaua and pass on the seriousness of their situation.

On the morning of 27 June Pouchain felt a bit better, and some of the crew attempted to release the ship from the trap. The engines worked at full power, all unnecessary items were thrown overboard, but they were still stuck. A request for as-

sistance was signalled again, the amount of 90% poisoned crewmen was specified in the report. Soon from Massaua the torpedo ship "Acerbi" set off to the rescue, she was supported by the destroyers "Pantera" and "Leone", but the latter soon turned back due to a failure. The purpose of the ships was to free "Perla", and if it was impossible, at least save her crew. The ships turned back at 1230 hrs, when Italian recce aircraft reported a strong force of the British ships, including a cruiser.

Two hours later, when the crewmen were still trying to free "Perla" from the trap, the enemy formation was sighted from the submarine: the New Zealand cruiser "Leander" and the British destroyers "Kingston" and "Kandahar", which immediately commenced rapid gun firing (according to Italian estimates, the distance was around 10,000 m). "Perla" replied from her gun, but it soon jammed.

In the face of a certain defeat and massacre of the crew the commander ordered to abandon ship. Burning of classified documents and evacuation of the crew commenced, some were to swim, part of them on a raft, the care of the sick was entrusted to sottotenente di vascello Vincenzi. Captain Mario Pouchain remained aboard, electrician Arduino Forgiarini refused to leave his skipper, soon the brave sailor was hit by a fragment and died, he posthumously received the *Medaglia d'Oro al Valor Militare*. The first mate, tenente di vascello Renzo Simoncini, who had come down

from the deck, still in a state of intense poisoning, went unnoticed again towards the ship, and died, trying to save the Regia Marina banner. 13 men died under fire.

At that time, another amazing turn of events took place in the story of "Perla". Eight SM.81 bomber planes appeared over the scene. Their presence prompted the British to stop attacking. The raft under the command of Vincenzi reached the shore, so did several swimmers. Unfortunately, some of the Italian seamen drowned. At sunset several men got back to the ship to collect water and food. On the order of the commander, guardiamarina Galla led the strongest men toward the Sciab Sciach lighthouse, which was located about seven miles from the beach on which they landed. On the next morning the destroyer "Manin" rescued the survivors. On the way to a safe harbour, the dead, whose corpses were found aboard the "Perla", were buried at sea. Among them, next to the mast with the flag flying, was Simoncini, who had previously been evacuated to the beach together with others!

In the following days, more expeditions were sent from "Massaua" to save the submarine. First, capitano di corvetta Spagone, commander of Flottiglia Sommergibili based in Massaua, found himself on board her. Spagone examined the submarine, analysed the extent of damage and decided on the measures needed to recover her. On 15 July another rescue expedition set off (command-

On 6 May 1941, „Guglielmotti" arrives in Bordeaux [„Storia Militare Dossier", No. 12] ed by Spagone). Technicians and labourers were working on the ship, they did their job at night in order not to draw the attention of enemy planes. The first task was to remove the water that flooded the hull and to tackle the battle damage. In the end, they managed to fix the damage and restore the ships floatability, and on 20 July "Perla" returned to Massaua on tow. There, the ship underwent the necessary repairs. At the time of the "Perla's" evacuation, a British tugboat and three destroyers were discovered near the Cap Ras Cosar; the SM.81s immediately attacked them.

In December 1940, the commander was changed, T.V. Pouchain was replaced by tenente di vascello Bruno Napp, also the navigator, sottotenente di vascello Vincenzi was replaced by guardiamarina Elio Sandroni, already familiar to us from "Macallè".

"Torricelli's" legendary duel

On 14 June, "Torricelli" (capitano di corvetta Salvatore Pelosi) left Massau with the task of replacing "Ferraris", which had a battery failure. On the way, the ship stopped for two days (16th and 17th) in Assaba, a port in the Bab-el-Mandeb Strait, an Italian possession since 1882 that was used as a bunker station. Some minor failures were fixed there.

On the morning of 19 June the submarine arrived in the area of Djibouti (French Somali), her designated sector. The sea was raging. Submarines of the Brin type performed poorly under such conditions, especially when waves hit the stern, resulting in the ship submerging halfway. In this case, the water, striking the conning tower

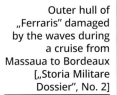

Outer hull of „Ferraris" damaged by the waves during a cruise from Massaua to Bordeaux [„Storia Militare Dossier", No. 2]

from the side of the gun, had a tendency to break through the open main hatch. In turn, below the deck, the temperature reached 45° C, and the air humidity approached 100%. In the evening came an order adjusting the operational area slightly more to the south, closer to the coast (the waters of Muscia islet), where the ship was to remain for several days. Pelosi was not delighted with such a change, the new area meant scattered shallows and rocks.

On 21 June the ship found herself in the indicated area. Soon, however, she was detected, attacked with depth charges and heavily damaged (probably by the sloop "Shoreham" or a joint action by the destroyers "Kingston" and "Khartoum"). According to Italian sources, the enemy clearly expected the "Torricelli", probably thanks to the documents taken from "Galilei". The British action caused such serious damage that Pelosi decided to return to base. The ship was speeding full ahead on the surface. Fuel was leaking and leaving a visible trail behind. At night on 22/23 June "Torricelli" had to overcome the most difficult obstacle, the Bab-el-Mandeb Strait, from 4 am patrolled by three destroyers and a sloop that were heading south-west. Probably a radio message sent from the ship was decoded. Again, it was possible due to the material acquired from the "Galilei".

In the early hours of 23 June "Evangelista Torricelli" remained in the area of the island of Perim (Bab-el-Mandeb Strait), and was sighted by the lookouts on HMS "Kingston", the Italians were then distant by about 3 NM. The destroyer moved towards the potential booty, which in the meantime went down under the water. Soon "Torricelli"

On 20 May 1941, „Perla" is greeted in Bordeaux, inter alia, by the German military band [„Storia Militare Dossier", No. 12]

was detected by ASDIC on the sloop "Shoreham" and attacked with depth charges. It is certain in the sequence of events, that the Italians managed to avoid detection and sneak out around 0430 hrs. Inaccurately, however, the extent of the damage is given, according to some references, the ship could not be submerged due to the failure of the ballast tanks[9]. Probably this crew also struggled with gas poisoning from a leaky air conditioning system. Pelosi ordered full ahead north-west, towards Assab, where he could find a refuge, because the port had a coastal artillery battery. Just a few minutes later, the Italians were spotted from "Kingston" again, the British, however, were positioned in the wrong place, now they had to rush behind the fleeing submarine.

About 0515 hrs "Torricelli" was surprised on the surface by three K-type destroyers ("Kandahar", "Kingston" and "Khartoum") and two sloops "Shoreham" and "Indus". At approximately 0530 hrs, the Italians opened fire from their only 100 mm gun (cannone da 100/42), they also had four 13.2 mm machine guns at their disposal. The advantage of the Italians in this engagement was their gun mounted at the back of the high conning tower, thanks to which they had a wide field of fire in the area behind their stern. Pelosi manoeuvred his ship with great expertise. The British commenced firing at 0536 hrs, altogether they had as many as 18 120 mm guns (each destroyer had six) and four 102 mm guns (two on each sloop), but sinking a single submarine took them about 40 minutes.

The Italians' fight in this situation had signs of suicide, but they moved on at full speed. Not only that, the Italians hit HMS "Shoreham" (1,105

t) many times, forcing her to leave for Aden. The columns of water began to fall behind the stern of the Italians, a glimmer of hope sparkled. However, the destroyers had already taken up suitable positions. Pelosi fired a full torpedo salvo at them from the aft launchers. The British destroyers made a turn to avoid torpedoes, and luckily they succeeded. This gave the Italians a moment's respite, but the enemy continued to push on, firing from 120 and 40 mm guns. During the duel, the spring of the gun's firing pin on the "Torricelli" was damaged so they had to use a hammer to shoot. The gun was often silent, but in the end it always responded with fire. The Italian 13.2 mm machine guns sprayed a hail of the bullets onto the decks of the destroyers.

The Italians concentrated their gunfire on the destroyer "Khartoum" (1,690 t). This most likely caused an Italian 100 mm shell fragment to pierce a compressed air cylinder of one of the torpedoes in the aft starboard tube. It was set on fire, which the crew failed to control. As the ship approached the small harbour on the island of Perim, the fire reached the aft ammunition magazine. The destroyer blew up. The explosion took place five hours after the fight, the ship was thrown into the shallows, which caused her total destruction. It is debatable whether it was actually an Italian success. Italian authors mock the argument that the event was not related to the fight, because every day ships of different fleets blow up all over the world. Alleged patrolling the Strait by the destroyer, which is supposed to justify her stay in the Perim area, also raises doubts. The ship would be visible to Italian observers on the coast and could fall victim to Italian planes deployed at the airfield around Assab. The island of Perim often experienced air raids, which made its anchorage deserted. British reports always raise a question mark, thanks to the C.A.F.O. (Confidential Admiralty Fleet Order) 2972/39 directive, ordering not to disclose, but only to inform the Admiralty, about damage suffered as a result of direct hits, which would occur as a result of Italian activities in the Mediterranean and the Red Sea. All other events were left to the discretion of the Mediterranean Fleet headquarters, which was to follow the Ministry of Information regulations regarding war propaganda. Put simply, there was a embargo imposed banning information on any Italian success, except for those which could not be concealed anymore (sinking/severe damage).

It was not until 0605 that "Torricelli" got the first hit - the rudder gear was damaged and the commander was wounded. Probably now the ship lost the ability to go underwater, she was also immobilized. Around 0610 hrs Pelosi ordered scuttling. The enemy was circling at a distance of several hundred metres, with the obvious intention of capturing "Torricelli". Firing was limited to machine guns, as the British did not want to lose the opportunity to get valuable documents intact. Earlier, despite the firing of 700 shells, the British did not manage to destroy the Italian ship.

After 10 minutes in the water, the first group of Italians, together with their seriously wounded commander, was taken aboard by "Kandahar", a second one by "Kingston". "Khartoum" took two men aboard. At 06.24 am "Torricelli" sank at 12° 34' N and 43° 16' E, and the last sign of her was the flag of Regia Marina disappearing under the surface of the Red Sea. Italian sailors in the water shouted spontaneous salutes saying goodbye to their ship.

Captain Geoffrey Kirkby from "Kingston" had counted on getting secret documents, and he managed to escape from the deck of a sinking ship at the last moment. He was awarded the Distinguished Service Cross (DSC).

The crew of "Torricelli" watched from the decks of the destroyers "Kandahar" and "Kingston", as "Khartoum" throws herself ashore on the island of Perim. After the fight Pelosi was received with full honours on board the "Kandahar" by Commander Robson. The Italian had lunch with the officers, and then he found out about the sinking of "Khartoum". Pelosi received the *Medaglia d'Oro al Valor Militare*. Two Italians perished in the sea during the fight, three died on board "Kingston", one on "Khartoum", and two more sailors from "Torricelli" died in captivity.

Tragic June

At the time of Italy's entry into the war, "Archimede" (tenente di vascello Elio Signorini) was in Massaua, where maintenance on her faulty air-conditioning system was carried out. The work was stopped suddenly, at the behest of the viceroy of Ethiopia, who believed that methyl chloride was not very harmful. On 19th June the ship put out to sea, her hunting area was the waters near Djibouti. The submarine was supposed to cooperate with "Perla" there. The mission ended before its designated time and in dramatic circumstances.

On the "Archimede", there was a leak of methyl chloride from the air conditioning system. Not even one full day of the cruise had passed, and the first men began to reveal symptoms of sickness. Initially, however, the reasons for these events were not recognized. The situation systematically deteriorated, at the end of the fourth day the air conditioning system was turned off. Two officers and several non-commissioned officers and seamen suffered heatstroke, and other submariners also showed symptoms of poisoning. Most of the crew suffered from depression and fainting initially and then on subsequent symptoms until some men were on the verge of death. There was an assassination attempt on board, other men falling into destructive madness. Finally, "Archimede" submerged to the bottom of the sea and spent all day near the Bab-el-Mandeb Strait.

Late on the afternoon of 23 June the commander began to seriously consider aborting the mission. The command in Massaua only responded by designating the ship's new position... by 50 NM more to the south. A tragedy occurred on 23/24 June, when four sailors died on board. Signorini immediately interrupted the patrol and took a return course, because of the further deterioration of the health of the crew members the ship headed to the nearest port of Assab. On 26 June at 8.30 am, "Archimede" arrived at this base. 24 men were seriously poisoned, including Captain Signorini and the chief mechanic, they were immediately disembarked. Sottocapo Luigi Zecchini and sailor Ermenegildo Rubini died after several hours, raising the number of fatal gas leak victims to six. Eight men went crazy and the rest fell ill for a long time. The patients spent five months in the Massaua hospital, and then got two weeks of rest in Asmara.

The ship herself from Assab, which was an auxiliary base without proper infrastructure, was manned back to Massaua by a healthy crew, under a temporary commander, capitano di corvetta Livio Piomarta, and a new chief mechanic, who was transported by the destroyer "Leone". "Archimede" left Assab on 3 July, on 5 July she was already in Massaua, and she was restored for service on 31 August. The deadly methyl chloride was replaced by much more reliable freon, but most of the Italian ships used the coolant for the following months. At that time the unfortunate Signorini was succeeded by capitano di corvetta Marino Salvatori.

In the first month of the war for the Red Sea, the "Ferraris" (capitano di corvetta Livio Piomarta)

"Guglielmotti" in camouflage pattern, which was painted in Massaua, moored in Bordeaux, May 1941 [„Storia Militare Dossier", No. 12]

also put to sea. On 10 June she left Massau with the task of taking up position in the waters near Djibouti. At night of 12/13, an enemy destroyer was sighted in the Bab-el-Mandeb Strait. Piomarta went underwater and prepared to attack. During this manoeuvre, it was noticed that water was flooding one of the battery packs, the reason for this was a ventilation valve left partially open. Then, the release of methyl chloride was discovered, which poisoned most of the crew. This failure could not be repaired at sea, so she returned to Massau on 14 June. Along the way, she was accidentally bombarded by Assab's coastal battery and slightly damaged. At this port, she spent the night of June 13/14. Let us indicate, immediately after her return on 15 June, the port of Massaua was the target of allied air raids. This was the grey everyday life of Italian sailors cut off in East Africa.

The period between 15 June and 10 August 1940 "Ferraris" spent at the dockyard in Massaua, where she underwent the necessary repairs. At that time, Piomarta commanded "Archimede" which returned from Assab to Massaua.

In the first operations, half of the submarines were lost. Many submariners went for shorter or longer treatments. Although there was good news here, the rest on the Tigray plateau, where the altitude exceeded 2,000 m above sea level, quickly put men on their feet. At the end of June, only "Guglielmotti" was operational. Positives were the infliction of losses on the enemy and the persistent and courageous attitude of the crews, which Italians would not have to be ashamed of when compared to any navy in the world.

No care was taken by the loss of "Galilei", even codes and ciphers were not changed. Operations indicated in the documents captured by the enemy were not continued, and this was due to the

extreme fatigue of the Italian forces in the first period of operation. The Italian sailors were exhausted by the prevailing heat, and their everyday lives were also ulcers.

Fruitless search

In July it was ordered that one ship was to be at sea, another to be ready for action, and the next two were to rest their crews and undergo maintenance. Apart from patrols in the Red Sea, it was also planned to go into the ocean, so that the enemy still had to take care of escorting his shipping there. The missions were to last a maximum of eight days, preferably four to five.

Enemy convoys avoided sailing in coastal waters, full of natural obstacles - shallows and rocks, and suitable for laying minefields, practically always one route was chosen, below the 18° parallel. Theoretically, it was possible to attempt a decisive blow against convoys steaming there, but Italian air reconnaissance was mediocre. The Italians had their Reheita observation post near the Bab-el-Mandeb Strait, but the enemy tried to move convoys there after sunset, when it was difficult to observe them effectively.

Men and ships were greatly affected by the climate. The equipment of the ships was already heavily worn, there were various failures, everything was practically irreparable. The situation deteriorated especially in December 1940, when the enemy was very active. At the end of the year, the head of Marisupao Adm. Balsamo was replaced by Adm. Bonetti. In December and January, only two ships put to sea, carrying out unsuccessful missions.

On 26 July "Guglielmotti" (capitano di corvetta Carlo Tucci) left Massaua to hunt in the area of the waters surrounding the island of Masamruh. They were looking for a merchantman sailing south of Suez. They did not discover anything and after three days returned to the base.

On 2 August "Guglielmotti" set off towards a designated hunting zone between the islands of Gebel Tair and Gebel Zucur (Hanish Islands). Again, the patrol turned out to be fruitless and on 5 August she returned to Massaua. On 21 August the ship set sail again and headed to the same area, she suffered a failure and after four days she returned to the base. On 23 August the HQ in Rome received information that two Greek merchantmen were sailing south. Six destroyers also took part in the search, but all efforts failed.

On the evening of 13 August the news reached Addis Ababa that an enemy battleship had passed Suez and headed south. Only two or three SM.81 were available for air recce. On the morning of 14 August "Ferraris" set out from Massaua. In the Bab-el-Mandeb Strait a zigzaging destroyer or small cruiser was seen and after taking up a suitable position at 2355 hrs on 15 August from a distance of 1,000 m, two torpedoes were fired against this ship[10]. Everything took place at a heavily turbulent sea, which was probably the reason for the inaccurate Italian torpedoes. "Ferraris" immediately descended to 85 m. The ship was subjected to about a three-hour attack with depth charges, but it managed to slip away underwater. "Ferraris" did not suffer any serious damage and on 19 August she returned to Massaua. There, she immediately survived an air raid by the Allied air force, suffering light damage. The target the ship was looking for was the British battleship "Royal Sovereign", which went from Suez, but managed to reach Aden on 17 August. She slipped through near the Arabian coast, avoiding shoals, mines and unauthorized eyes.

On 25 August "Ferraris" left Massaua for hunting between Gebel Tair and Gebel Zucur. She did not sight the enemy and on 1 September returned to the base. During this cruise, an enemy cruiser was being sought heading for Suez. She was attacked with 100 kg bombs by four Italian bombers, a search by two destroyers also failed.

On 31 August a message came from Rome sent by the military intelligence service S.I.M. that a convoy of 20 ships was on its way from Bombay to Aden, which was to arrive on the same day. Its further route was not clear, it could pass through the Red Sea or circumnavigate Africa, so the message was also passed on to the Germans. Air and naval forces were warned by A.O.I. Reconnaissance flights were performed throughout the day.

On 3 September "Guglielmotti" set out to hunt between the island of Dahlak and the Arabian coast. On 5 September contradictory information began to arrive: in the morning, five freighters sailing in the company of a cruiser to the north were signalled from the Raheita observation post. This message reached the Admiralty only at noon. In the meantime, the air force reported eight freighters and two cruisers heading south, too far away to be intercepted by Italian ships. "Ferraris" was directed north of the island of Harmil (she stayed at sea between 5-8 September, the patrol was ineffective).

At midday one of the planes sighted a group of ships steaming at an estimated course of 315°. There were supposed to be 30 ships, accompanied by three destroyers heading for Suez (convoy BN 4). It was near the area where "Guglielmotti" was operating. The Italian destroyers had already returned to sea, but the weather deteriorated, visibility was poor.

At 1530 hrs a few Italian planes attacked the convoy to the north of the Dahlak archipelago. Later, the convoy was probably directed toward the Arabian coasts, bypassing the areas patrolled by "Guglielmotti" and "Ferraris" and avoiding the night search by Italian destroyers. Only one of the British destroyers fired a torpedo in the darkness at a target identified as an enemy destroyer.

The enemy could not be found the next day either. The destroyers returned to Massaua. At

„Ferraris" during maneuvering at the port of Bordeaux [„Storia Militare Dossier", No. 12]

1300 hrs capitano di corvetta Carlo Tucci saw two ships through his periscope. One of them quickly went out of range and sailed away. The second target looked like a tanker which was in a suitable position. A Greek flag was visible on her mast. Two torpedoes were fired from a distance of 700 m, which hit the port side between midship and bow, leading to a leak of the cargo of fuel, which was not accompanied by a fire. The crew left the deck and retreated to a small island located nearby, later it was evacuated to Aden. There were no losses. Tucci watched as that the ship had a bow trim, but it she did not go down, so he fired a third torpedo, but its course was disturbed by waves in the rough sea. A fourth torpedo hit the port side again, the tanker began to sink with her bow down, breaking apart at the same time. The bow sank, the aft part kept floating all the time. The tugs "Hercules" and "Goliath" tried to bring her to Suez, but because of the wind and the stormy sea, the tow parted and the stern of the ship sank between the Egyptian town of Barnis (Berenice) and Cape Ras Banas. The victim was the tanker "Atlas" (4,008 GRT), sunk in the neighborhood of the Arab Farasan islands. Greece was still neutral at the time, but the ship was sailing for the British and was a missing vessel from the convoy BN 4. The Greeks sailed from Abadan to Suez, but remained behind the convoy. Some sources report that the ship had already been damaged by aircraft.

On 17 September a new opportunity arose to intercept the enemy convoy. Headquarters sent the government in Addis Ababa and the latter to Marisupao the following signal: on 11 September a convoy from Singapore set off carrying 4,000 troops, including two battalions that previously served in China. The ships were supposed to sail at a speed of 15 kn without stopping in Bombay, and head for Port Sudan. The escort, nine ships including a cruiser and four destroyers, were to replenish supplies 150 NM east of Socotra, from ships which were to arrive there from Aden. In Massaua it was calculated that the convoy would not reach the Bab-el-Mandeb Strait by 20 September. Air reconnaissance, two submarines and destroyers were prepared for this occasion. On 19 September one of the planes located the BN 5 convoy in the waters of the Indian Ocean, its composition of 21 freighters in the company of a cruiser and two destroyers was signalled. The force was south-east of Aden, heading for the Bab-el-Mandeb Strait.

On 19 September "Guglielmotti" left Massaua to search for the reported convoy. "Archimede" did the same. On 20 September the convoy was attacked by Italian aircraft in the morning and afternoon. Four destroyers left Massaua which were to intercept the convoy at night. The Raheita observation station signalled the passage of a second convoy accompanied by an auxiliary cruiser. At night, contact was lost, aerial reconnaissance

Skipper of „Perla" tenente di vascello Napp interviewed by Admiral Angelo Parona [„Storia Militare Dossier", No. 12]

was not carried out, and the Italian destroyers with no radars sought without result and on 21st returned to Massaua.

On the morning of 21 September "Guglielmotti" sighted a convoy of four freighters in the company of two cruisers and two destroyers. Because of its position it had to be another convoy or only part of a large convoy observed by the air force near Aden (19 September). The distance was so great that "Guglielomtti" could not get anywhere near the enemy and take up a favourable position to attack. Only the signal about the discovery was sent out. The enemy was too strong for the Italian destroyers during daylight, and it was too fast to catch up with it at night. Italian planes did not maintain contact, and "Archimede" did not observe anything. "Guglielmotti" returned to base on 22 September.

The last patrols

On the morning of 5 October "Archimede" left Massau as part of an ordinary patrol against the enemy's shipping. During the day, the air force observed a convoy near the Bab-el-Mandeb Strait, which was steaming at a speed of 12 kn on a course of 315°. The message was immediately sent to the submarine, and in the evening two destroyers left Massau. The monsoon heavily disturbed the surface of the water, a thick and low cloud curtain concealed the sky. The dark night fell quickly. Due to the state of the sea, the Italian destroyers limited their speed to 16 kn. "Archimede" was subjected to shocks all the time, various items were flying around under the hatches. The lookouts were only able to see something just a few hundred meters away. The enemy convoy managed to pass undetected.

On the evening of 18 October the Raheita observation post observed in the Bab-el-Mandeb Strait five steamers in the escort of a cruiser and four destroyers. The alarm was raised, at dawn the first recce plane took off. Admiral Balsamo ordered that in the morning two submarines would set off out to sea, at noon the destroyers would follow and after dusk they should reach the estimated position of the convoy to the north of Massaua. It was a large group of ships that sailed from the Indian Ocean to Port Sudan and Suez.

In the morning, the planes discovered the enemy, but it turned out that he was steaming at a greater speed than expected, around 16m kn and was therefore much further than it had been assumed. The destroyers were unable to catch the convoy. "Guglielmotti" also left Massaua. In fact, the BN 7 convoy was also more numerous, it was made up of 31 steamers divided into groups. The escort consisted of the cruiser "Leander", a destroyer and five sloops. At 2200 hrs a new message was sent from Raheita: 23 steamers passing through the strait in front of the Italian outpost, accompanied by a cruiser and four destroyers, estimated speed 10 kn. The destroyers were to be prepared at noon the next day. The "Ferraris" was supposed to be ready to leave port in the morning.

On 20 October at 11.00 am the convoy was attacked, despite the presence of Allied aircraft, by a sole SM.79. During the attack, the wireless on the Savoia bomber was damaged, so the alarm was only raised after its landing, around 12.30. The composition of the convoy matched the report from Raheita. A few minutes after the return of the plane, "Ferraris" left Massaua (she returned on 23rd). Four destroyers also put out to sea.

"Guglielmotti" managed to find the convoy. According to the commander's report, two destroyers (in fact sloops) were sighted. The enemy was also alerted, the British rushed at the Italians and drove them under water. "Guglielmotti" descended on 100 m. For several hours, the enemy was heard, and then sailed away without dropping depth charges. The submarine, however, lost contact with the convoy and returned to Massau on 24 October. Then capitano di corvetta Tucci was replaced by capitano di fregata Gino Spagnone, commanding officer of the Italian submarines in the Red Sea.

On 22 November "Archimede" was at sea again and looking for a reported convoy. After four days of searching, the ship turned back and on 27th came to Massaua. At the end of November, a patrol was also carried out by "Ferraris". Between 24-28 November she was patrolling in the Red Sea, also she was looking for a report-ed convoy. "Ferraris" reported the torpedoing of three freighters on 26 November 1940. The enemy did not confirm any hit by the Italians. In the early morning that day, merchantmen were seen escorted by light cruisers and destroyers. The speed of the enemy was estimated at 7 kn. Capitano di corvetta Piomarta partly submerged the ship, leaving the conning tower above water and prepared torpedo tubes nos. 1, 3 and 4. Using a moment of inattention by one of the destroyers which made a gap in the escort formation, he fired at a distance of 700 m. "Ferraris" immediately went down into the depths. Under the water, two explosions were heard, and after a long time also a third, much louder.

On 3-8 December (Masamaruh Island waters), on December 23-30, 1940 (near Port Sudan), and on 20-26 1941 (between Gebel Tair and Gebel Zebair), "Ferraris" performed other fruitless patrols. During the last of them, a hospital ship was noticed, which of course was not attacked.

On 12 December "Archimede" reached its designated hunting zone between the Dahlak Archipelago and the Farasan Islands. Again no targets were detected. On 16 December she returned to base. On 18 December "Archimede" left Massaua to patrol along the 18° parallel. No shipping was discovered and on the 22nd she returned to base. On 12 January 1941, the same ship patrolled along the Arabian coastline. Again she discovered nothing and returned to Massau after four days.

On 2 February "Archimede" set out for the waters near Aden. The ship approached a convoy of 39 freighters under the escort of a cruiser, destroyer and five sloops. "Archimede" did not make contact, at night the convoy was attacked by Italian destroyers. After a few days, she returned to base.

Evacuation of the Red Sea

In the winter of 1941, it became almost certain that Massaua would fall into the hands of the enemy. It was necessary to think about the further fate of the ships stationed there. Of the four submarines that survived by this time, the worst situation was on "Perla". The ocean-going submarines could even try to reach Japan. At that time, the smallest one was to be sent to Madagascar, the Vichy possession in order to get interned. Finally, it was decided, in agreement with Admiral Karl Dönitz, that the Italian ships would try to reach the Italian Betasom base in Bordeaux. It was planned to rebuild the double bottom of the ships so that they could take more fuel, but eventually the dealings with the Germans were made. It was feared how the exhausted men would respond to the equatorial climate and uninterrupted voyages lasting more than two months. During this period, difficult conditions at sea were to be expected. All

20 May 1941, „Perla"
in Bordeaux [„Storia
Militare Dossier",
No. 12]

the time it was necessary to take into account the failures of the weary machines, especially the batteries functioned in an emergency, to a different extent it was a problem for all submarines. Similar problems were also caused by the on-board distillers. Massaua had only modest means to remedy this situation. On 28 February 1941, orders were issued to evacuate the ships to Bordeaux. Spare torpedoes were not taken on board.

If unable to re-fuel at sea, "Perla" was supposed to do so in Madagascar and the larger ships in Brazil, the Canary Islands or Cadiz. Another concept was final offensive missions and then to seek internment in neutral ports. In emergency situations, decision-making was left to the commanders.

As always, British intelligence and its decryption service were reliable. "Ultra" already knew on 1 March 1941 about the planned cruise, got to know the details of the planned route and knew about the planned supply of ships at sea. However, the enemy did not know exactly the location of

Beirut, July 1942, „Perla" photographed a few days after her capture. The ship fought a duel with corvette HMS „Hyacint", as a result of which she was captured by the British. She was listed in the Royal Navy as P 712 and tested, and eventually sold to the Greek navy, where the ship served until 1954 as „Matrozos" [„Storia Militare Dossier", No. 3]

the zone in which the Italians would be supplied, which is why a search was conducted by HMS Severn (Operation "Grab"). She was assisted by the auxiliary cruiser "Alcantara" and the sloop "Milford".

All ships passed the Bab-el-Mandeb Strait under water. Larger ships came across a rough sea and a strong wind in the Mozambique Channel, between Madagascar and Africa. Whenever a lonely ship was seen, it was passed under water. After refuelling from the German supply vessel "Nordmark", the ships passed a considerable distance from the Azores and headed east towards Bordeaux.

On 3 March "Ferraris" left Massaua. On 21 March a violent typhoon caused damage to the stern. On 10 April the Italians were seen from the deck of HMS "Severn". At 1947 hrs, four torpedoes were fired at them, at 1950 another two, all turned out to be inaccurate and unaware of any-

thing "Ferraris" sailed farther and farther. North of the Tristan da Cunha Archipelago, she collected supplies from the German tanker "Nordmark". On 9 May 1941, she reached Bordeaux[11]. Piomarta received *Medaglia d'Argento al Valor Militare*. Between 15 May and 1 October, she went through a major overhaul, a lot of effort was devoted especially to bringing the diesels to full efficiency. On 25 October 1941, near Gibraltar, the ship was damaged by a plane. The "Ferraris", which could not go underwater, fought with the destroyer "Lamerton" which had arrived in the meantime. She was scuttled by her crew.

"Archimede" ended the Red Sea stage of her career by a cruise from Massaua to French port of Bordeaux between 3 March and 7 May 1941. North of the Tristan da Cunha Archipelago she collected supplies from the German tanker "Nordmark". In Bordeaux, the ship was reviewed and the crew rested after a long voyage. She later succeeded in the Atlantic. On 15 June 1942, she sank the Panamanian steamer "Cardina" (5,586 BRT) and the British motorship "Oronsay" (20,043 BRT). She was sunk on 15 April 1943 by US planes.

On 4 March the "Guglielmotti" was the last to leave from Massaua to Bordeaux. Her radio mast was damaged near Madagascar, and contact with Betasom was lost. Sailors Cuomo and Paolo Costagliola (participant in the expedition which saved the ship "Macallè") volunteered, secured only with a cable wrapped around their waists, in reached the edge of the stern and made repairs. They were both thrown off the deck by the raging sea, but they always managed to return to it, at the same time suffering various injuries and wounds. Both received the *Medaglia di Bronzo al Valor Militarei* for their courage[12]. North of the Tristan da Cunha Archipelago, the ship collected supplies from the German tanker "Nordmark". On 6 May she reached Betasom and went through the necessary repairs[13]. On 15 March 1942, she was sunk in the Mediterranean by the British submarine "Unbeaten".

As the first, on 1 March 1941, the port of Massaua was left by "Perla" (tenente di vascello Bruno Napp), the smallest of the four to try to reach Bordeaux. The ship was still undergoing renovation works, difficult due to the isolation of East Africa, there was no efficient water distiller on board. It was not known how a small coastal submarine would perform during such a long voyage through two oceans. The time required for the passage of "Perla" from Massau to Bordeaux was estimated at approximately three months. The ship was only briefly repaired after her previous adventures. "Perla" had never performed a comparable mission in the ocean. Wind and sea could disrupt the planned route of this small ship, excessive fuel consumption could have occurred, the internal combustion engines could malfunction due to changes in temperature and humidity.

All unnecessary equipment was removed, including reserve torpedoes. An incomplete crew also set off on the cruise. These measures were necessary to embark the largest possible supply of food and fuel. The commander also received a clear order not to perform any offensive actions. This applied to all ships going to France that were supposed to stay away from popular shipping routes. The entire operation was to be carried out in strict secrecy, and ships at all costs were to avoid detection, also by neutral vessels. "Perla" soon after leaving the port was attacked with depth charges by a Bristol "Blenheim" plane. Fortunately, there was no damage and further pursuit of the Italians.

The route of "Perli" led through the Bab al-Mandab Strait, which was passed under the water, as well as the intensively patrolled Red Sea, then most of the way was covered on the surface. Then, alongside the island of Socotra, the ship got into the open waters of the Indian Ocean, circling Madagascar from the east, to avoid the often bad weather in the Mozambique Canal. They were afraid of not getting a fuel supply, so "Perla" travelled most of the way at economic speed. For this reason the cruise was quite slow.

On the way to France, the ship had to refuel twice, fortunately in the Indian Ocean there was the German auxiliary cruiser "Atlantis" (Cdr. Bernhardt Rogge), which met with various supply vessels. For the first time, "Perla" planned to take on fuel and other supplies at a point about 450 NM south-east of Cape Cap Sainte Marie (now Cap Vohimena), at the southern tip of Madagascar. It was not until 28 March that the German raider was encountered. "Atlantis" was at that time disguised as the Norwegian ship "Temesis" (7,256 GRT). At night, 70 tons of fuel, oil, water and food were taken aboard, followed by a further cruise along the Cape of Good Hope.

They kept a good distance from the shores of hostile South Africa. Later she set a course to the west-west northwest and sailed into the Atlantic,

passing between Tristan da Cunha and St. Helena. On 16 April three larger ships reached the meeting point marked with the code name "Andalusia", around 20° S and 20° W; 4,000 NM from the meeting place "Perla" with "Atlantis". The German tanker "Nordmark" was already waiting there, masquerading as the Vichy ship "San Pedro". It was not until 23 April although according to the schedule, "Perla" reached the "Andalusia" sector, having overcome the "roaring forties" region with problems. In addition, only one of the diesel engines was used to save fuel.

Then "Perla" sailed between Natal and Freetown, leaving Cape Verde on her starboard, avoiding the busy routes, and then turned north to the archipelago towards the Bay of Biscay. The journey continued without interruption. "Perla", after 81 days at sea, reached Betasom on 20 May 1941, having covered 13,100 NM. The story of the Italian submarines in the Red Sea ended with this considerable feat. The ship was unfit for service in the Atlantic. On 20 September "Perla" again put to sea, on the 28th she managed to sneak past Gibraltar (on the surface, along the coast of Africa), and on 3 October reached Cagliari.

Bibliography

E. Bagnasco, M. Brecia, *I sommergibili italiani 1940-1943 - Parte 2 - Oceani*, Albertelli Edizioni Speciali S.R.L., Parma 2014.

C. Capone, *Siamo fieri di voi*, Istituto Grafico Editoriale Italiano, Naples 1996.

E. Cernuschi, *La rivalita anglo-italiana nel Mar Rosso*, [in:] Storia Militare Issues Nos. 16 and 17 Ed. E. Bagnasco.

W. Holicki, *Klęska erytrejskich dywizjonów*, [in:] Morze Statki i Okręty Issue No. 6/2008 Ed. A. Jaskuła.

D. Lembo, *La Regia Marina fuori dal Mediterraneo*, IBN Editore, Rome.

R. Nassigh, *Guerra negli abissi - I sommergibili italiani nel Secondo conflicto mondiale*, Mursia, Milan 2013.

V. Meleca, *Storie di uomini, di navi e di guerra nel Mar delle Dahlak*, Greco&Greco editori, Milan 2012.

Endnotes

1. Silver Medal For Military Valour
2. D. Lembo, *La Regia Marina fuori dal Mediterraneo*, IBN Editore, Rome, p. 23.
3. According to some references, „Galilei" broke the radio silence. The signal was intercepted aboard the "Kandahar", and the pursuit was on the trail again. Italian historians do not mention such an event.
4. Some discrepancies are demonstrated by references, sometimes they mention about a slight poisoning, sometimes about a serious one, and it is sometimes even questioned at all.
5. In fact, in the Royal Navy itself classified her as a sloop, and in the literature she also is described as a gunboat or an advice-boat.
6. D. Lembo, *La Regia Marina...*, p. 16.
7. Gold Medal For Military Valour, the most important Italian military decoration.
8. C. Capone, *Siamo fieri di voi*, Istituto Grafico Editoriale Italiano, Naples 1996, p. 253.
9. Such a failure occurred indeed, but slightly later.
10. It was probably one of the destroyers escorting the battleship - "Dainty", "Defender" or "Decoy".
11. She covered 14,000 NM in 68 days.
12. Bronze Medal For Military Valour.
13. 12,425 NM in 66 days.

The Escort Aircraft Carrier

Casablanca Type

The CVE-58, 1944, Pacific

Drawings
Sławomir Zajączkowski

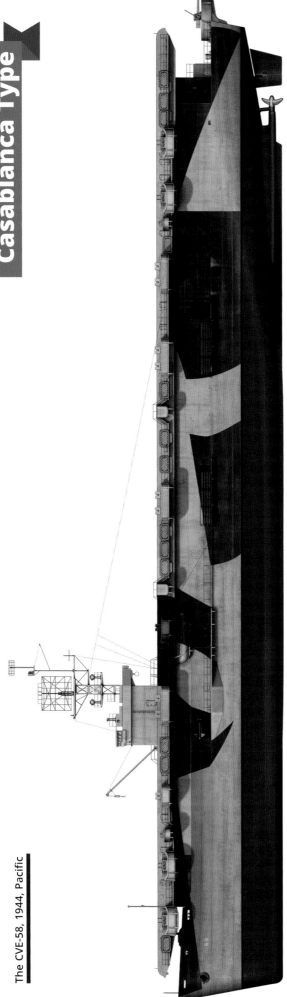

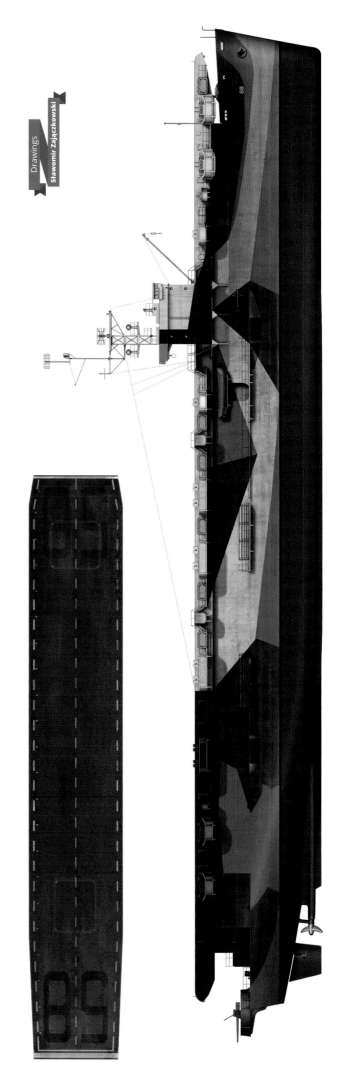

CVE-69 from the end of 1944, the Mediterranean

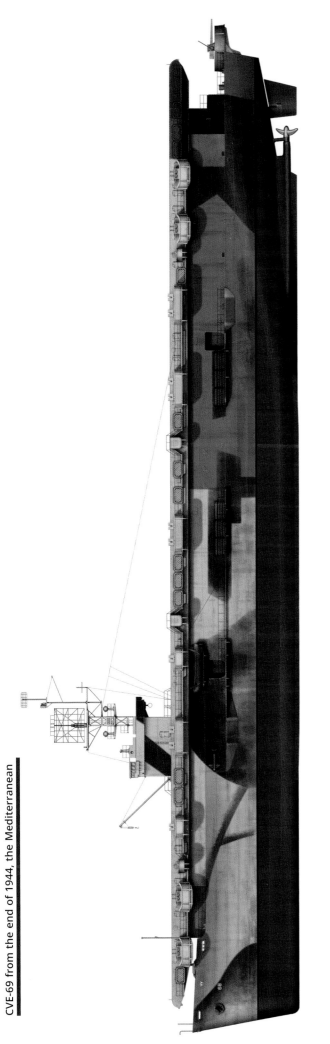

Drawings
Sławomir Zajączkowski

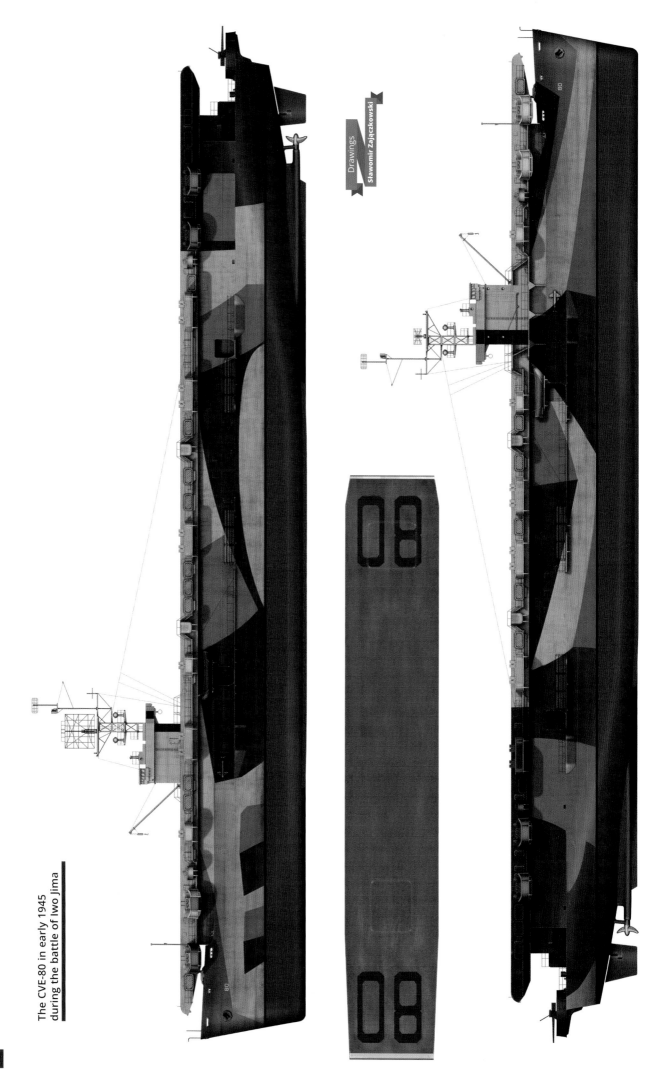

The CVE-80 in early 1945
during the battle of Iwo Jima

Drawings
Sławomir Zajączkowski

The CVE-78 from a period of
the Battle of Leyte Gulf, 1944

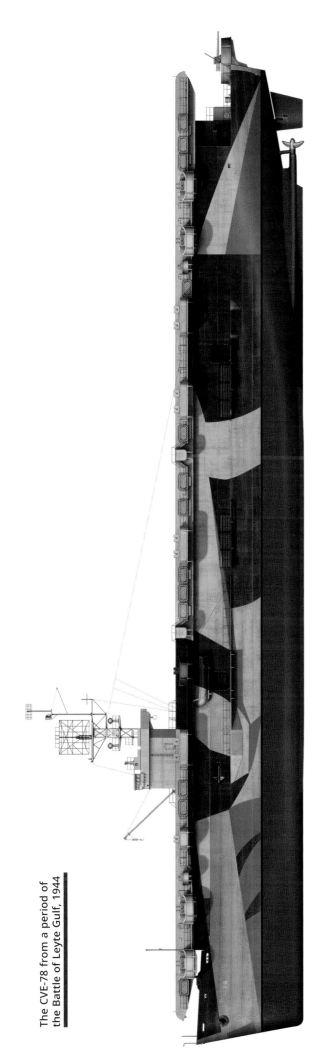

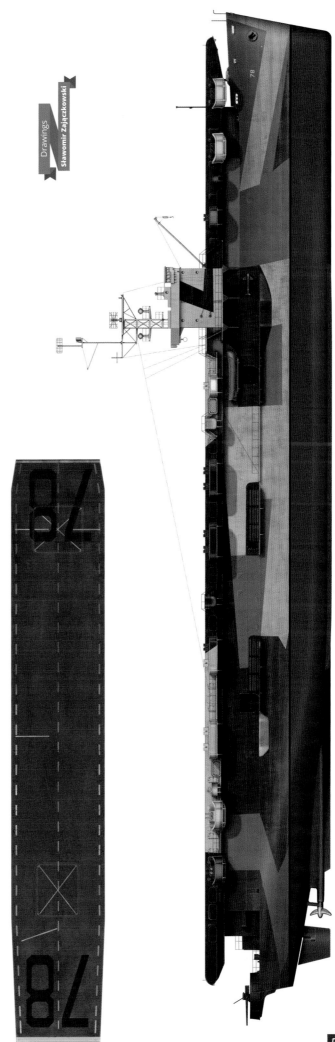

Drawings
Sławomir Zajączkowski

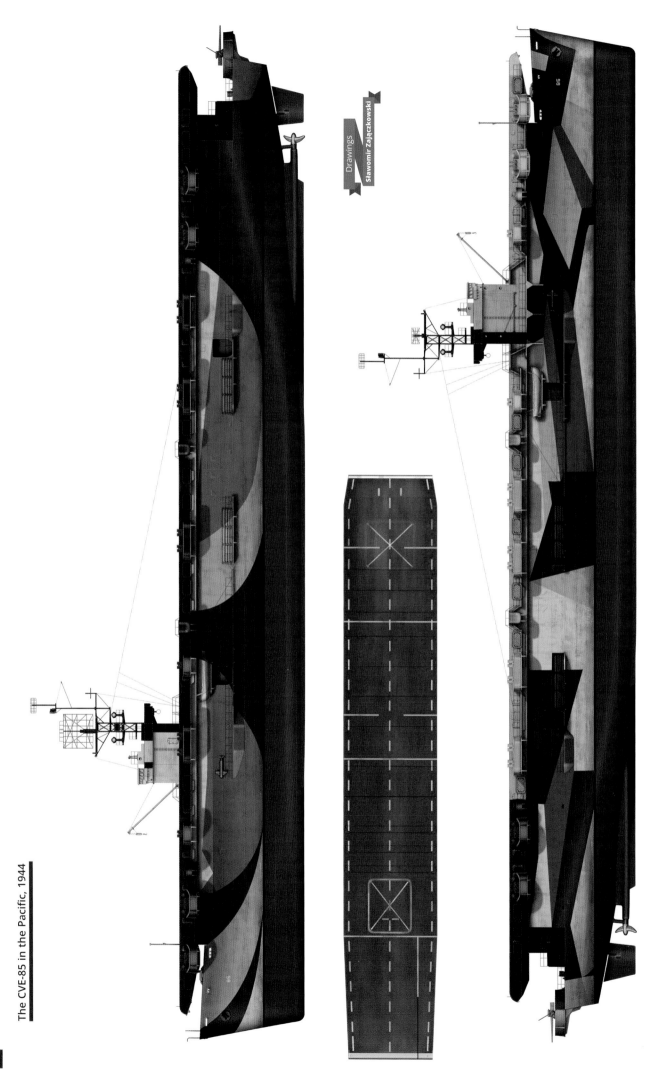

The CVE-85 in the Pacific, 1944

Drawings

Sławomir Zajączkowski

The CVE-94 participated in the battles of Iwo Jima as well as Okinawa, 1945

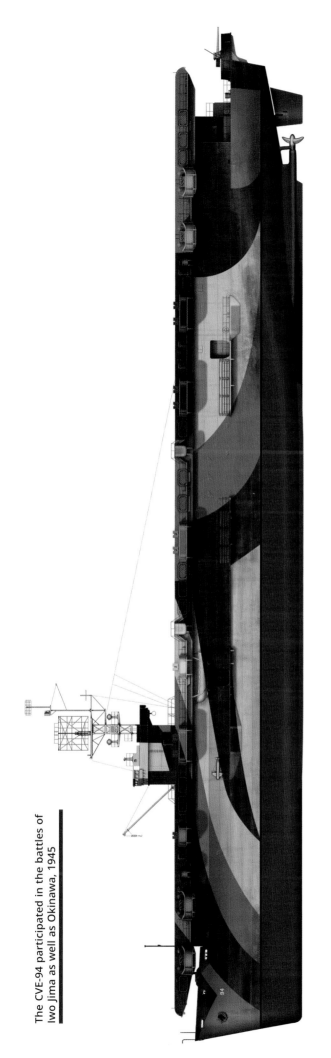

Drawings
Sławomir Zajączkowski

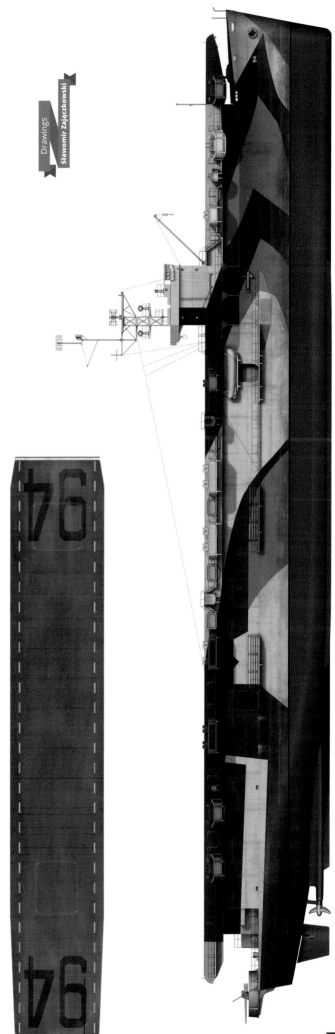

Super-destroyers Of The Sovremenny Type (Project 956 "Sarytch")

Jan Radziemski

A Project 956 destroyer fires a RBU-6000 ["Military Parade"]

The Sovremenny type destroyers represent the third and so far the last generation of Russian ships of this class. They had been built from 1976 for over a dozen years, once they were one of the showpieces of the Soviet fleet. Equipped with a turbosteam turbine, which was a phenomenon on a global scale, because of this solution most of them ended their maritime career prematurely. Currently, there are six destroyers of this type in the Russian Federation Navy: three in the line, two in reserve, and one ship is undergoing a planned refurbishment. The merits of these large and beautiful ships were appreciated by the Chinese Navy, which has purchased four vessels of this type. In this way they became the largest surface warships ships exported by Russia.

Origins

The death of Stalin in 1953 and the taking over of power by Nikita Khrushchev and his associates pushed the development of the USSR's fleet in new directions. The missile era had arrived, preceded by the slaughter of large surface warships. All fleet development programmes of the Stalinist times were abandoned, construction of large gun-armed ships was stopped, and almost finished cruisers were sent for scrap. Intensive development of submarine forces had begun. Surface ships were in disgrace, unless they could be armed with long-range missiles, such as destroyers and then Project 58 cruisers. But not a decade passed, before there was a need for large surface warships again. This resulted both from the needs of the navy, such as to cover the deployment of its own strategic submarines, as well as reacting to the actions of the enemy. At that time, the US Navy had at least 15 aircraft carrier strike groups (ASG), about 40 strategic nuclear submarines and many large surface warships, such as battleships, helicopter carriers, cruisers etc. Needless to say, all these forces operated in the open spaces of world's oceans. The implementation of tasks for which the Soviet fleet was responsible, required maintaining at least 80-100 ocean-going surface vessels of high sea worthiness and autonomy. And these were few and far between. A partial solution to this problem turned out to be the construction of large anti-submarine warships (Projects 1123, 1134A, 1134B), which protected the deployment of strategic submarine forces, as well as having the ability to track enemy "boomers". Unfortunately, their combat capabilities were limited in terms of defence against missiles and large gun-armed ships. They required the cover of other ships. The shortage of escort forces in the oceanic

Destroyer
"Vdumtchivy" (690)
[MoD RF]

zone became fully obvious during the large ma-noeuvres called "Okyean" in April 1970.

When in the mid-1960s the Soviet navy introduced the so-called full-time combat service performed by surface vessels, it turned out that for lack of alternatives old Project 68bis cruisers and Project 56 destroyers (and even Project 26 bis cruisers as well as Project 30 bis destroyers) were directed to it. Although the latter can hardly be called ocean-going vessels. Despite ageing, thanks to high speed and powerful guns, they could perform ASG tracking. Medium-calibre guns also came back into favour. It was considered that it had prospects for further development, for example as a means of destroying coastal targets and combating small sea- and airborne targets over shorter distances. Their guns were not enough, however, anti-ship missiles were needed. In connection with this, other ships (including nuclear strike submarines) had to be involved in tracking the ASGs. At the same time, it turned out that the old cruisers and destroyers, which were doomed to fail against the mighty opponent, could nevertheless prove useful. The destroyers of Project 56 mentioned above, due to their speed, could constantly follow US aircraft carriers, and in the event of a military conflict (commenced by the USSR) within 10-15 minutes of engagement, until their destruction, could even cause serious damage to an aircraft carrier[1]. The strategic war game "Horizon" carried out at the Naval Academy in 1970 scientifically confirmed the conclusions accomplished by the sailors after the "Okyean" manoeuvres. One of them was the need to design a multi-purpose destroyer[2].

Design stage

The project of such a ship was contemplated for the first time in 1969. The study work was carried out at the Central Research and Development Institute of the Ministry of Defence (CRDI MoD) of the USSR, as well as at the Northern Construction Office (formerly CKB-53). At the initial stage of work on the preliminary draft, numerous combinations of weaponry were considered in connection with two types of ship propulsion unit, namely: turbo-steam and combined diesel-tur-bogas. The basic variants of the ship at this stage of design referred to Project 1134, equipping it with new types of weapons: 130-millimetre guns, "Kub" type anti-aircraft guided missiles, anti-ship missiles and numerous variants of power unit. The constructors took into account the solutions used by the US Navy on the destroyers F. Sherman (DD 931) and partly Charles F. Adams (DDG-2). The basic task of the ship at all stages of discussing tactical and technical goals remained "fire support of the amphibious landing", and its basic armament was medium-calibre guns. However, as work progressed and more information about the US competitors was obtained, the new ship gradually began to expand its combat tasks, which led to classifying it as a universal gun-armed ship.

Another important task of the ship was to provide anti-aircraft defence when sailing the high seas, and therefore the missile complex "Uragan" (instead of "Kub") appeared. As for the main gun, there was the single-barrel A-217 130 mm gun (ZIF-92 factory index). Work on it had been carried out since June 1967 at the Construction Of-

fice of the "Arsenał" Works. The trial piece was tested in 1974, but it did not achieve the expected rate of fire 60 rounds/minute (actually just 45), and the weight of the entire unit exceeded the planned one by 10 tons. The results were predicted earlier, which is why as early as in 1970 work on the twin-barrel option started[3]. As a result, the A-218 (ZIF-94) was introduced.

The preliminary design variant of the new ship, armed with three A-217 guns, developed by V. A. Konoplev, served as the basis for the further design of the destroyer. The main elements: a hull, one funnel, two masts and two groups of superstructures would be preserved until the end of the design process. As a result of all these works and discussions, tactical and technical requirements (TTR) were formulated for the design of a new destroyer, which were approved on 31 December 1970 by the Minister of Shipbuilding (on 8 January 1971, accepted by Admiral Gorshkov). According to the TTR, the ship was to perform the following tasks: destruction of small-size ground targets, fire support and anti-aircraft defence in the landing area, destruction of the enemy's surface vessels. To accomplish these tasks, the ship was to be armed with, among others: two or three universal A-217 cal. 130 mm guns, "Uragan" anti-aircraft missiles (one launcher), two RBU-6000 and two RBU-1000 throwers. In addition, the possibility of installing two twin-barrel AK-130 mounts was considered. Finally, it was recommended to consider the possibility of equipping the ship with four P-15M missiles to engage surface targets. The ship's displacement was determined at 5,000 t, and speed at 30-32 knots. The matter of the ship's drive unit system had not yet been decided.

On behalf of the TTR, the Northern Construction Bureau undertook to develop a preliminary design. In January 1971 K. A. Maslennikov was appointed the main designer of the new ship project.

It was given the number 956 and the code "Sarytch"[4]. A total of 13 variants of the preliminary project were created, which were meticulously assessed from a military and economic point of view. The effectiveness of two basic tasks was considered: fire support of amphibious forces and the task of tracking enemy combat forces of surface ships in the distant waters.

The subsequent design process was complicated by the introduction of the US Navy multirole destroyer "Raymond D. Spruance" on the other side of the ocean (commenced in 1972). It resulted in the change of purpose of the Soviet counterpart, which from now on would be transformed into a multi-purpose ship. Above all, it was ultimately decided to use the multi-channel "Uragan" anti-aircraft complex, but its location was changed (now at the bow and stern) in order to improve its sectors of fire. The ship's striking abilities were also significantly strengthened by choosing eight state-of-the-art surface-to-surface missiles of the "Moskit" complex (instead of the four missiles originally planned for the P-15M "Termit" complex). It was also decided to take a risk by choosing the AK-130 mm automatic gun, even though it was not ready yet. The constructors were kept awake at night by the ability of defending against submarines. The means were modest to say the least. Due to the large dimensions of the new "Polinom" hydroacoustic station (the weight of the antenna itself was 800 t) it could not be installed on the ship without a drastic increase in displacement. So there was a standard set to choose from: two RBU-1000 launchers and only two twin-tube 533 mm torpedo launchers plus a temporarily-based Ka-27 helicopter in a folding hangar located amidships. Instead of the large "Polinom" station, it was proposed to install a small "Plátina-S" hydroacoustic system with an antenna placed in a bow bulb. To compensate for the weakness in armament, Admiral Gorshkov

Table No. 1. Comparison of "Sovremenny" and the U.S. Navy destroyers			
	Sovremenny	Spruance (DDG-963)	Kidd (DDG-993)
Combat readiness of the first ship of the series	1980	1975	1981
Specifications			
Displacement. t			
- standard	6500	5930 (empty)	6950 (empty)
- full	7940	7909	9574
- maximum	8480	8040 (in 1988)	
Dimensions. m			
- Overall length/(waterline)	156.5/145	171.7/161.2	171.7/161.2
- Overall beam/(waterline)	17.2/16.8	16.8/16.8	16.8/16.8
- Draft/(waterline)	8.2/6	8.8/5.8	10/6.2
Top speed. kn	32	33	33
Range. NM/kn	4500/18	6000/20	8000/17
Type of power unit	Turbo steam	Turbo gas	Turbo gas
Output. HP. number of shafts	100.000 2	86.000 2	86.000 2
Crew (officers)	344 (25)	319 (20)	363 (31)
Armament			
Rakietowe			
- strike	8 x *Moskit* (8)	8 x *Harpoon* (8)	8 *Harpoon* (8)
- A-A	Complex *Uragan* 2×1 (48)	*Sea Sparrow* 1×8 (24)	*Standard* 2×2 (52 A-A and 16 ASROC
- ASW	2 RBU-1000 (48)	ASROC 1 × 8 (24)	See above
Guns	2×2 130 mm AK-130 (2000) 4 x 6 30 mm AK-630M (16.000)	1×127 mm Mk 45 (1.200). 2×6 20 mm *Vulcan/Phalanx* (36,000)	2×127 mm Mk 45 (1.200). 2×6 20-mm *Vulcan/Phalanx* (36,000)
Torpedo	2×2 533 mm (4)	2×3 324 mm (14)	
Aircraft	1 Ka-27	2 SH-2 or 1 SH-3D	2 SH-2 or 1 SH-3D
Radars	*Fregat-M* or *Fregat-M2*	SPS-40. SPS-55	Sps-48. SPS-55
Hydroacoustic station	Platina-S	SQS-53	SQS-53A. SQR-19

suggested an original solution. He proposed a system consisting of a pair of ships working together, one of which with powerful surface-to-surface armament ("Moskit" complex) and the other with sophisticated ASW equipment. The latter was supposed to be the large anti-submarine warship for Project 1155 "Fregat".

The preliminary project was ready in 1972, and the type of power plant was selected at the technical design stage. Two propositions submitted in the preliminary design were selected: a gas turbine and a turbo steam turbine. The former had an economic advantage (about 20%) and weight indicators (less fuel, less weight and volume, which allowed reduction of the full displacement of the ship by almost 1,000 tons). The latter variant of the drive ensured much lower operating costs (using much cheaper fuel, less complicated and expensive maintenance). In the end, it was decided to use a turbo steam power unit, not so much for tactical or economic reasons, but mainly for production factors. It was feared that the plants currently producing gas turbines for several ship series would not be able to meet the needs of all recipients. On the other hand, the plants producing traditional steam turbines would have spare capacity. In addition, it was assumed that during the serial production it would be possible to increase the economics of the steam turbine and reduce its size by using flow boilers instead of boilers with natural circulation.

The technical project was submitted for approval on 27 June 1973. Interestingly, up to this point there was no officially appointed chief designer. The general management over the design process was held by the head of the Central Construction Bureau No. 53 A. K. Perkov, the chief engineer. V. F. Anikiyev and the head of the design department M. A. Ostroumov, and specific problems were dealt with by I. I. Rubis and J. T. Vasilyev. It was not until the summer of 1973 that Anikiyev was declared the main designer of the Project 956.

The completion of the technical project did not mean the commencement of studies on the working documentation and the beginning of the construction of the destroyers. There were permanent corrections and clarifications. The matter of fire control system of the "Moskit" complex ("Mineral") and aircraft equipment was discussed. In May 1977, due to the lack of new KWG-1 boilers, they were replaced by older KWN98/64-PM ones, and this required another alteration of the design. Six months later, the main designer of the Project 956 was changed. Anikiyev was replaced by Igor I. Rubis, who had actually run the project from 1969. Equipping the destroyer with two AK-130 turrets and a helipad for a Ka-27 with a hangar significantly changed the profile of ship in comparison with the initial design variant[5]. In July 1977, the standard displacement at the level of 6,500 t was finally determined, full – 7,940 t

	Name	Construction No.	Keel laid	Launching	Date of acceptance	Commissioning	Attached to
				No. 190 "A.A. Zhdanov" Shipyard in Leningrad			
1	Sovremenny	861	03.03.1976	18.11.1978	25.12.1980	24.01.1981	NF
2	Otcayanny	862	04.03.1977	29.03.1980	30.09.1982	24.11.1982	NF
3	Otlitchny	863	22.04.1978	21.03.1981	29.09.1983	15.12.1983	NF
4	Osmotritelny	864	27.10.1978	24.05.1982	30.09.1984	07.12.1984	POF
5	Byezupretchny	865	28.01.1981	25.07.1983	06.11.1985	07.01.1986	NF
6	Boyevoy	866	26.03.1982	04.08.1984	28.09.1986	05.11.1986	POF
7	Stoyky	867	28.09.1982	27.07.1985	30.12.1986	24.02.1987	POF
8	Okrylenny	868	16.04.1983	31.05.1986	30.12.1987	19.02.1988	NF
9	Burny	869	04.11.1983	30.12.1986	30.09.1988	09.11.1988	POF
10	Gryemyashtchy	870	23.11.1984	30.05.1987	30.12.1988	01.05.1989	NF
11	Bystry	871	19.10.1985	28.11.1987	30.09.1989	31.10.1989	POF
12	Rastoropny	872	15.08.1986	04.06.1988	30.12.1989	28.02.1990	NF
13	Byezboyaznennyj	873	08.01.1987	18.02.1989	28.11.1990	29.12.1990	POF
14	Byezuderzhny	874	24.02.1987	30.09.1989	25.06.1991	11.07.1991	NF
15	Byespokoyny	875	18.04.1987	09.06.1990	28.12.1991	11.02.1992	BF
16	Nastoytchyvy (ex Moskovskyi Komsomolets)	876	07.04.1988	19.01.1991	28.12.1992	05.02.1993	BF
17	Byesstrashny	877	06.05.1988	28.12.1991	30.12.1993	21.01.1994	NF
18	Vazhny	878	04.11.1992	23.05.1994[1]	25.12.1999	Sold to China	
19	Vdumtchivy	879	19.04.1993	28.03.1999[1]	25.11.2000	As above	
				No. 200 "61st kommunar" Shipyard in Nikolaev			
20	Vnushitelny	2211	30.08.1983	17.10.1987	Not completed		

Table No. 2. Construction of the Project 956 destroyers

1 – official information for China

(1.6 times higher than stated by the TTR) and maximum - 8,480 t. Meanwhile, the construction of the first ship was already carried out at a high rate. According to the new classification of ships (adopted in 1977), it became a first rank destroyer. Its task was to strike the enemy surface ships, fire support of the amphibious operations, as well as anti-aircraft and anti-ship defence of the force's war ships and transports.

Construction and tests

The construction of the destroyers of Project 956 was carried out by shipyard No. 190 "A. A. Zhdanov" (later Severnaya Vyerf - Northern Shipyard) in Leningrad (later St. Petersburg). Beginning the construction required over 24,000 working drawings (in 1981 there were almost 32,000 of them). Their number resulted from the complicated technological process of building destroyers. The ship was divided into nine sections and

as many building blocks. The ship's construction process was carried out successively in three locations. The keel of the first Project 956 destroyer - "Sovremenny" - was laid on 3 March 1976. The assembly of the hull took place in the first open location was performed on a slipway, and indoors, in the other two locations, the assembly of boilers, main and auxiliary mechanisms took place, superstructures were installed, cables were laid etc. The hull was assembled from sections with the block forming, starting from engine-boiler compartments towards both the bow and stern. The weight of the sections ranged from 35 (deck and broadside) to 50 (bottom) tons. The construction technology provided for the aggregate method of assembly of mechanisms. The modular-aggregate method proved to be too complicated for the shipyard unprepared for such a novelty. In fact, instead of 141 aggregates, only 79 were assembled, and from the planned 141 assembly blocks there was... one! Launching the hull took place at the

"Otlitchny" in June 1983 [MoD Bonn, courtesy of John Jordan]

Table No. 3. Comparison of the "Moskit" complex and "Harpoon" system		
	"Moskit" (1984)	"Harpoon" RGM-84 (1980)
1 Range, km	90 (120)	120
2 Altitude, m	Up to 20	3–20
3 GSN search sector, degrees	+/- 60	+/- 60
4 Warhead weight, kg	300	227
5 Overal missile weight, kg	4200	667
6 Top speed	M>2	M = 0.84
7 Overall length, mm	9400	4630
8 Diameter with folded wings, mm	1300	340

technological readiness of about 70% in the so-called Russian way, using a floating dock.

Despite these complications, the pace of the series construction was fast. In 1986, two ships were transferred to the navy per year. Initially, 50 destroyers were planned to be built. Implementation of the entire programme was to cost around 2.1-2.5 billion roubles. The price of a series production ship at the preliminary design stage (1971) was estimated at 47-51.5 million roubles. By the technical design stage (1974), it increased to 75.1 million roubles, but in 1976 (after adjusting the technical design and detailing the costs of the entire program), the quantity of destroyers was limited to 32 ships. At the end of 1988, the cost of each destroyer was already over 100 million roubles, which led to another cut in the quantity down to 20 ships. The collapse of the USSR caused the programme to be abandoned. Up until 1991, the Soviet VMF received 14 ships of this type. Three more vessels have been completed for the Russian Navy already ("Bespokoyny", "Nastoytchivy" and "Besstrashny"). In total, 17 destroyers had been built, not counting the four ships sold later to China. In order to accelerate the pace of construction of the Project 956 destroyers, it was decided to involve the Black Sea shipyard to contribute, the "61st Kommunard" shipyard in Nikolaev. Construction of the first ship - the "Vnushitelny" - began in 1983. The construction was swaying relentlessly, so that the launching took place only on 17 October 1987, but it did not come to its final completion. The hull then played the role of a floating shipyard warehouse. The second hull was cut into scrap on the slipway. According to other information, the construction of the second ship did not take place at all.

"Byezupretchny" [MoD UK, courtesy of John Jordan]

"Boyevoy", 1986
[MoD Bonn, courtesy
of John Jordan]

In the construction process, destroyers were constantly modified. Starting from the number 867 ("Stoyky"), main boilers were changed for more modern ones. The "Fregat-M" (MR-710M) radars were installed on "Sovremenny", "Otchay-anny" and "Otlitchny". On the destroyers numbered 864 and 865 ("Osmotritelny" and "Bezu-pryeczny") a newer version of the "Fregat-M" radar with one flat and one parabolic antenna "Fregat-M1" (MR-710M-1) was fitted, and on the others the "Fregat-M2" (MR-7) 750) with two flat antennas. In addition, from the seventh destroyer of the series ("Stoyky"), the ships received a modernized variant of the "Uragan" complex with 9M317 missiles (which increased their displacement by 100 t). From the twelfth destroyer of the series ("Rastoropny"), a modernized variant of the "Moskit-M" missile complex with 3M-82 missiles was installed. The destroyer "Okrylny" (handed over to the navy on 30 December 1987) was covered with a special substance absorbing electromagnetic waves and hindering the detection of the ship.

Acceptance tests

The shipyard tests lasted from 5 August to 13 November 1980, and state tests from 16 November to 25 December 1980 in the region of Liepaja and Baltyisk. It was then that the new destroyer was first observed by NATO ships and given the call-sign "Balcom-2". The tests took place without armament, because the plants had not managed to deliver it on time. During the measured mile tests, the displacement (additional fuel was supplied) was slightly higher than the normal one – 7,305 tons. With an average displacement of 7,250 t, the ship reached a top speed of 32.7 knots, while the

starboard engine achieved the output of 50,300 hp and 298 rpm, and the port side engine 49,300 hp at 297 rpm. Mr. A.S. Pavlov's statement about the speed of 41 knots is pure fantasy. The armament tests were carried out according to a shortened programme because many systems were not yet ready. In total, the ship spent 143 days on trials, sailing 8,485 NM. Signing the act of acceptance of the ship on 25 December 1980, however, did not mean that the ship would enter service with the VMF of the USSR. For, among other things, fitting of the gun fire control system MR-184, "Uragan" and "Moskit" complexes etc had not yet been completed. After installation of the said systems, in January 1981 the ship went to the Far North in order to carry out further tests. She returned to Liepaja and on 30 December 1981 set off to the Black Sea for missile tests of the anti-aircraft complex. The stay in the south lasted until the end of July 1982. During the trials, not everything went as planned. For example, during the AK-130 tests, a barrel of the fore turret was torn open and its fragments damaged the bridge. Only luck must be attributed to the lack of victims. It was not until 6 August 1982, when she arrived in Severomorsk, she was actually ready to enter service.

Technical description

Architecture
The ships had large, wide (atypical for destroyers) hulls, designed on the basis of the hulls of cruisers Project 1134 and 1134A. The hull length coefficient was 8.7[6]. Thanks to this, they featured good sea worthiness in rough seas, although they required greater engine output (about 20-25%), especially at speeds above 20 knots. A well pro-

Table No. 4. Comparison of the "Uragan" (USSR) and "Standard" SM-1 MR (USA) missiles		
		Uragan (1983)	*Standard SM-1MR* (1983)
1	Guidance system	AG + SRA-G	IS RS + SRA-G
2	Targets engaged simultaneously. pcs.	6	2-4
3	Firing zone. degrees	360	360
4.	Top distance of a target. km - Airplanes. helicopters - Winged missiles	 18 6	 15-20
5	Target altitude zone. m - Airplanes - Winged missiles - Helicopters	 15–15,000 10–10,000 >15	 15–20,000
6	Top speed of a target. m/s - Airplanes - Winged missiles - Helicopters	 420–830 330–830 <140	 600–680
7	Reaction type (standby mode). s	16-19	10
8	Range zone. km - aircraft above 1000 m ceiling - aircraft below 1000 m ceiling - winged missiles	 3.5–25 3.5–18 3.5–12	 3–46
9	Missile weight. kg	690	640
10	Warhead weight. kg	70	61
11	Missile dimensions. m - length - diameter	 5.55 0.4	 4.5 0.34

Abbreviations:
AG – automatic guidance
SRA-G – semi-active radiolocation auto-guidance
IS – inertial system
RS – radiocommand system

filed shape of the hull, with the saddlecity of the fore part of the deck and strongly tilted frames in the bow area above the waterline, ensured a "dry foredeck - half-deck" even at a sea state of 6-7 degrees. It also made it possible to achieve the optimal angles of fire of the forward AK-130 gun. The hull was divided by fifteen bulkheads into sixteen watertight compartments. The large inner hull volume, estimated at 27,000 m2 (approximately corresponding to American standards adopted, for example, on the Kidd type destroyers), also allows location of the majority of combat posts inside the hull. The vessels of Project 956 have six decks located parallel to the waterline: the sec-

Stern of the destroyer "Sovreemenny" with 130 mm gun turret [MoD UK, courtesy of John Jordan]

Table No. 5. Comparison of the Soviet AK-130 and US Mk 45 guns			
		AK-130 (1987)	Mk 45 Mod. 3 (1982)
1	Calibre, mm	130	127
2	Number of barrels	2	1
3	Loading system	composite, automatic	Composite, automatic
4	Barrel type	monobloc	–
5	Barrel length, mm	6990	–
6	Barrel length, calibres	54	54
7	Lock type	Vertical, wedge-shaped	
8	Range, m	23,000	23,000
9	Altitude, m	15,000	13,600
10	Combat rate of fire, r/min	20–90 (both barrels)	16–20 (10 GR)
11	Weight of a round, kg	33.4	32 (47.5 GR)
12	Muzzle velocity, m/s	850	762–808
13	Weight of a mount (w/o ammunition), kg	98,000	22,200
14.	Elevation/traverse	-12, +80, +/- 180	-15, +65, +/- 170
15	Elevation/traverse speed, degrees/sec.	25/25	20/30

GR – guided rounds

The fore AK-130 mount of the destroyer "Byezupretchny", Portsmouth, 9 July 1990 [John Jordan]

ond, third and upper, half-deck, two platforms, one of which goes smoothly into the double bottom. The main hull constructions, reinforcements and foundations were made of steel with a low content of alloy components, and in areas of the highest stress - steel with increased plasticity. From the stern to the engine room compartment, two longitudinal bulkheads were arranged to provide additional rigidity to the aft part of the hull. As a result, there is no stern vibration at all speeds, which provides excellent conditions for the aft 130 mm gun. Another characteristic feature of the ship's hull is the large number of straight-walled sections that increase its radiolocation

echo (the surface of the ship's side is up to 1,700 m2). The ships were adapted to conduct operations in the nuclear-biological-chemical weapons environment, although long rows of side portholes that provide light to the crew's quarters probably make it difficult, and indeed much, to maintain the tightness of the ship. There are two large blocks of superstructures: fore and aft. The fore one is surmounted with a foremast (it serves as the mount for the heavy antennas of the radiolocation stations), and the aft part consists of a block with a funnel and a folding hangar, on which a light truss mainmast is located. The latter includes only antennas of communication devices and recce

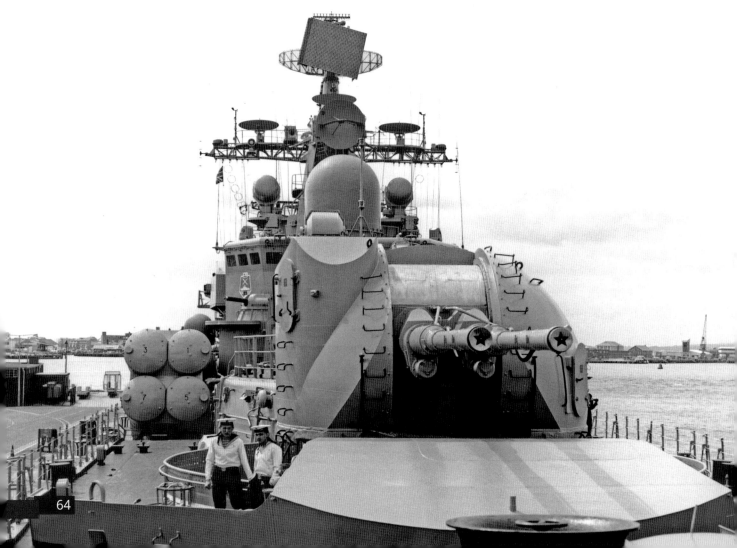

	Table No. 6. Comparison of the Soviet AK-630M and US "Vulcan/Phalanx" systems		
		Ak-630M (1980)	*Vulcan/Phalanx* Mk 15, Block 0 (1980)
1	Calibre, mm	30	20
2	Number of barrels	6	
3	Loading system	Composite, automatic	
4	Barrel length, calibres	54	53
5	Range, m	5,000–5,500	5,000
6	Altitude, m	2,500	2,500
7	Combat rate of fire, rounds/min	4,500	3,000
8	Number of cartridges ready for automatic firing	3,000	980
9	Weight of a round, kg	0.39	0.12–0.132
10	Muzzle velocity, m/s	1,050	832–1,030
11	Weight of a mount (w/o ammunition, kg	3,800	5,420 (together with fire control system)
12	Elevation/traverse	-12, +85, +/-180	-12, +80, +/-155
13	Elevation/traverse speed, degrees/sec.	50/70	92/126

systems. The superstructures of the ship were made of aluminium-magnesium alloy and connected to the hull with rivets.

Power unit

The propulsion of the ship is a twin-shaft turbo steam turbine located in two autonomous boiler-engine compartments. They are separated by a compartment with a turbogenerator and a compartment with boiler water tanks and a compartment with rooms for monitoring the operation of the power unit. In each compartment there are two boilers and one set of turbines with auxiliary mechanisms. The first six vessels had high-pressure boilers type KWN-98/64 installed, producing 98 tons of steam/h with a pressure of 64 kgs/cm2. The next ships were equipped with the KVG-3 boilers and TNA-4 turbochargers, more modern and reliable with a capacity of 100 tons of steam/h and a pressure of 66 kgs/cm2 at a temperature of 460-475° C. The weight of the boiler without water is 36-37.5 tons. Boilers of this type allow for very quick changes in power output and acceleration, for example, Project 956 destroyers can increase speed from 10 to 32 knots in just two minutes[7]! Steam produced by boilers is fed into two sets of GTZA-674 turbines of 50,000 hp each. Each set includes high and low pressure turbines. The backward motion turbine fits into the low pressure turbine hull. The fore GTZA is

the starboard engine and the aft GTZA is the port side one. The turbines transfer the power to drive shafts terminated with 4-blade variable pitch propellers via reducers. Design speed is 32 knots, on tests - 33.4 knots, economic speed 18 knots. The fuel capacity of 1,740 tons ensures a range of 4,500 NM/18 kn. The ships have one semi-balanced rudder.

Electricity is generated by two turbine generators of AK-1V type with a capacity of 1,200 kWt and four reserve diesel generators type DGAS-600/I with a capacity of 600 kWt each. The generators meet all the ships' requirements for three-phase alternating current with frequency 50 Hz and voltage of 400 V. The ships have two machines for desalination of sea water P 4-2 type. Autonomy, taking into account food supplies, is 30 days.

Armament

The "Moskit" missile complex

The main attack armament of the Project 956 destroyers is the "Moskit" missile complex. The missiles are placed in two quadruple launchers with a fixed angle of elevation, covered with anti-fragment plating. The missile reserve is eight units (in launchers). The KT-190 launch containers have a cylindrical shape. Work on this supersonic low-flying tactical anti-ship missile began in 1973 at the "Raduga" Construction Bureau. It was

"Byespokoyny" (620) - flagship of the Baltic Fleet [MoD RF]

"Osmotritelny" in
the Pacific in 1985
[RAAF, courtesy of
John Jordan]

supposed to replace the subsonic P-15 (P-15U) anti-ship missile. Tests of the first P-270 missiles (3M80) of the "Moskit" complex were carried out in 1981 on the destroyer "Sovremenny" and in 1984, it was approved by the navy. Serial production of missiles and their modified variants took place at the "Progress" plant in the Far East.

The 3M80 missile of the "Moskit" complex is designed to engage surface warships and transports with displacement up to 20,000 tons moving at speeds up to 100 knots, in the conditions of fire and radio-electronic countermeasures of the opponent, in all environmental conditions.

It should also be resistant to the effects of a nuclear explosion. The missile was made according to the aerodynamic design with folding X-shaped wings and a tail made of titanium. There are four lateral air inlets on the spindle-shaped fuselage with an oval nose part. The missile is propelled by a ramjet sustainer engine, inside which there is a powder starting engine with a working time of 3-4 seconds. The "Moskit" flies at a speed of 2,500 km/h, and just before hitting a target even at 2,800 km/h. The range is about 90 (120) km, this distance is covered in two minutes. The combined on-board missile guidance system includes an inertial navigation system, a radio altimeter and an active-passive radiolocation auto-homing head, ensuring the guidance of the missile during the last stage of flight, including under radio-electronic countermeasures conditions. Such a homing head has the ability to separate the target from a dipole cloud when the receiving part of the active-passive head is used to guide the interfering emission source. After launch, the rocket rises and then lowers its height to about 20 metres - this altitude is maintained throughout the entire sustainer section of the trajectory of flight. At the approach to the target, the "Moskit" descends to 7 m, just above the waves. In order to defeat anti-aircraft defences, the missile can perform a "snake" manoeuvre with turn angles of up to 60° and an overload of over 10 G, which ends at a distance of 9 km from the target. Due to the huge kinetic energy, the "Moskit" pierces the hull of the ship and explodes inside. Such a blow can sink a ship the size of a cruiser. The probability of hitting is 0.94 in the case of convoys and amphibious forces and 0.99 for the purposes of the type of cutter team or naval strike force.

Fire control of the "Moskit" complex is provided by the "Monolit" radar complex ("Mineral", KRS-27) that tracks the surface targets in both active and passive mode. Its antenna is hidden under a semi-spherical dome placed on top of the combat bridge. The passive mode allows it to "see" the target outside the radar horizon line. As a radiolocation station, general observation is provided by "Fregat-M" (on the first four ships of the series) and "Fregat-MA" (on the others). Fire control and correction of the trajectory of the rocket's flight (in the case of engaging objectives located behind the horizon) can be performed from a Tu-95C aircraft, a Ka-25C helicopter, a helicopter-ship recognition and indication "Uspyech" complex or satellites of the "Legend" space reconnaissance system. The "Moskit" missile complex, next to the missiles, includes: 3C80 guidance system, a launcher, on-board maintenance system and other elements. The time of readiness - from the moment of loading the missile to the launch of the first one - is 50 s. From the standby stage, during salvo fire the interval is 5 s. The ship's Weapons Management System allows performing a salvo from all eight launchers within 30 s after indicating a target.

The modernized "Moskit-M" complex was installed on the destroyer "Rastoropny" and all subsequent ones. Work on the modernized 3M82 missile variant with an increased range of up to 120 km began in the early 1980s. "Moskit" has no counterparts in the world. Thanks to the high speed, peculiar flight profile and the ability to perform deception manoeuvres, it is practically impossible for it to be destroyed by modern anti-missile measures. A serious drawback of the rocket is insufficient range. Flight at low altitude

with supersonic speed causes high air resistance, which limits the range to about 90 km. In addition, "Moskit" features considerable dimensions and weight: the length of the rocket is 9.38 m, weight 3,950 kg.

The "Uragan" anti-aircraft complex

The basic anti-aircraft armament of the destroyers is the multi-purpose, multi-channel, medium-range missile complex M-22 "Uragan". It covers escorted ships and individual defence of the carrier ship against simultaneous attack from various directions carried out by anti-ship missiles and aircraft. Work on the M-22 complex for the navy began in early 1972 at the Industrial Union "Altair". The basis for its design was the land-based complex 9K37 "Buk". Trials of the complex were carried out in 1974-1976 on the destroyer "Provorny" (Project 61E). In 1983, the M-22 was accepted by the VMF together with a 9M38 missile, unified

One of the destroyers of Project 956 in dock [MoD RF]

Fore superstructure of the destroyer "Byespokoyny" [MoD RF]

Two Project 956 destroyers before scrapping, in the foreground is "Boyevoy" (720) [MoD RF]

with the land-based complex. The 9M38 rockets (equivalent to the US "Standard" MR0 type) are launched from two single-rail MS-196 launchers (MoD index 3S90) with the missiles suspended underneath. Launchers are placed on the bow (foredeck superstructure) and on the stern behind the helipad. The weight of each launcher is 96 tons, the missile reserve - 48 rounds – is stored in special rotating drums under the launchers with two concentric rows of vertically arranged guides, intended for holding 24 rockets. The weight of the launcher without missiles is 30 tons. The complex allows it to engage 4-6 targets simultaneously at a ceiling from 10 to 1,000 metres at a distance of up to 25 km, and at an altitude from 25 m up to 12 km. The rate of launching missiles is one every 6-12 seconds. Top speed of the engaged target is up to 830 m/s. The probability of hitting an aircraft with a salvo of two rockets is from 0.81 to 0.96, with a winged rocket from 0.43 to 0.86. The complex uses a one-stage 9M38 missile, universal for army and navy. The missile has a solid fuel motor (operation time about 15 seconds), which gives it speeds to up to 1200 m/s. The missile can manoeuvre with an overload of up to 19 G. It is equipped with a semi-active homing head, autopilot, active-impulsive and contact fuses and a fragmentation warhead. It takes 16 seconds to prepare the rocket for launch from the moment a target is detected. Target missile guidance is carried out by means of proportional navigation according to the semi-active radar target tracking signal, which has an on-board calculator. Three missiles can be guided at one target at one time. The missile's radius of striking a target is 17 m. A contact fuse is used for engaging surface targets.

The destroyer "Vyedushtchy" (404) [MoD RF]

The complex does not have its own radar target detection station, it receives data from the three-coordinate general surveillance station, which allows it to shorten the reaction time (from the moment the target is detected to the missile launch) up to 6 seconds. The ships' 3R-90 (or 3R91) missile control systems consist of a computing system and six reflectors (radars) to illuminate targets of Oryekh type, placed three on each side of the ship. This makes possible to simultaneously track six airborne targets flying in from different directions. The reflectors are controlled by a guidance system receiving the coordinates of the targets from the "Fregat" radar. To achieve a standby status of the complex from the "cold" mode does not exceed three minutes. During a battle, the complex can operate in automatic mode or with centralized control of the entire control system of anti-aircraft defence. The "Uragan" ensures stable operation regardless of the time of day, in any weather conditions and sea conditions up to 5 degrees. Starting from the destroyer "Stoyky" (seventh in the series) a modernized version - the "Uragan-Tornado" complex - with new 9M38M/M1 missiles was installed (fire control system 3R91 type). The motor of the new missile has a longer operating time, which provides a greater range and speed of flight, the fire control system of the projectile itself was also changed and its resistance to interference was increased. The "Uragan-Tornado" complex has an increased range of up to 40 km, and the minimum altitude of a target has been reduced to 5 m[8].

The guns

The ships were equipped with powerful gun weaponry in the form of two twin-barrel 130 mm AK-130 guns and quick-firing cannons of smaller calibres, which is the last stage of the ship's anti-aircraft and anti-missile defence. The multi-purpose automatic cal. 130 mm guns are used to engage surface, coastal and airborne targets, including anti-ship missiles. An experimental specimen of the gun was prepared by the "Arsenal" Plant in 1976, but only in 1987 (according to other data in 1985), after a long process of bringing the design to specification, the 130 mm calibre turret entered service with the navy[9]. Each of the A-218 mounts is placed in a lightly armoured steel turret with a mechanism for feeding fixed cartridges from a magazine located underneath. Automated ammunition delivery and barrel cooling with water allows it to fire at a rate of 30 to 90 shots per minute over a distance of 23 km. Rate of fire is adjustable from single shots (salvo at the same time with two or one barrel shots) to continuous fire. Automation of loading and feeding of ammunition allows it to sustain fire at full rate until the ammunition is spent. The total weight of the unit is 98 tons, and the crew is six men. The gun fires fixed ammunition specially designed for it. The weight of a complete round of any type is 52.8 kg. Three types of cartridges are used: HE and two anti-aircraft (one of them with a radio proximity fuse). A round weighs 33.4 kg with 3.56 kg of explosives and muzzle velocity is 850 m/s. The choice of cartridge types and setting the radius of fuse activation takes place remotely in the automatic mode, providing a practical rate of fire which equals the rate of the mechanism. The supply of cartridges from the magazine to the mechanism is carried out in clips of two cartridges by means of elevators. In each turret there are 180 ready-to-use cartridges, the rest is stored in the 40-ton automatic loading complex. The total reserve is 500 cartridges per barrel. Presence of all these "wonders" of technology causes the massive weight of the post, so it can only be mounted on ships with a displacement of over 6,000 t. The disadvantage is the lack of guided gun rounds (GGR), which are available for the US Mk 45 type gun. Fire control takes place with the "Lew-218" multichannel system. The system consists of three elements: a radiolocator type MR-184 with an integrated television viewfinder with a range of 75 km, laser rangefinder "Lew-218M", TV viewfinder MR-184M. Each turret has optical sights of "Kondensor-218" type in case of failure or destruction of the main system.

The self-defence of the ship against low-flying aircraft and helicopters and missiles in the near vicinity is secured by two batteries of small-calibre anti-aircraft gun complexes (one on each side) in a set of two AK-630M mounts and one fire control system MR-123 "Vympyel". Each battery is equipped with two 30 mm AK-630 guns constructed in 1974 on the basis of the AO-18 weapon with a rotating block of six barrels, cooled with water. The rate of fire is up to 4,500 rounds/min. The AK-630M was adopted for service in 1980. It increased the set of ready-to-fire cartridges to 3,000 units. Fire control of the AK-630 is carried out only remotely by the MR-123 radar or optical sight. The theoretical probability of one AK-630 battery destroying a "Harpoon" missile in the mid-1970s was estimated at 0.4-1.0. Soviet specialists claimed that a battery composed of two AK-630s, even with lower radar capabilities and large weight, had an capability similar to one 20 millimetre "Vulcan/Phalanx" mount.

Anti-submarine weapons

Ships of the Sovremenny type have been equipped with a standard set of ASW weapons. Its main element is the medium-frequency hull-mounted active-passive MG-335 "Platyna-S" hydrolocator with a range of 10-15 km. Its antenna is located in the nose of the ship's bow bulb. The basic and practically the only (next to the helicopter) weaponry for fighting submarines are two twin-tube

torpedo launchers of 533 mm calibre called DTA-53, mounted amidships on both sides. All types of electric, guided ASW torpedoes are used, as well as those to engage surface ships. The basic type of torpedo is the SET-65. Another element of this modest ASW set are two 6-barrel throwers for rocket depth charges RBU-1000 ("Smertch-3") type. They are located at the stern part, on the aft superstructure. The RBU throwers are used to engage submarines at short distances and depths, and destroy torpedoes heading towards the ship. The 300 millimetre launchers, loaded automatically, have a firing range from 125 to 1,000 m. Fire control is provided by the "Purga-956" complex. In the aft part of the deck, the ship has mine tracks, and in the stern transom two compartments have been set up with devices that allow mines to be set. The ship can take on board up to 22 mines of different types[10].

Aircraft equipment

The destroyers are equipped with a helicopter landing pad and a folding hangar. The Ka-27 helicopter was designed to be temporarily based on the ship. The folding, small and tight hangar does not ensure proper conditions for maintenance. A small supply of aviation fuel (5 tons) is enough for two refuelling operations. The landing pad at the centre of the ship does not enjoy the accolade of pilots who prefer to operate from helipads located on the sterns of ships. The helicopter is used to conduct radio-electronic reconnaissance and to indicate targets for the 3M80 anti-ship missile complex "Moskit". It can also be used to combat enemy submarines within the area of the anti-aircraft security zone of the ship.

The heavy Ka-27 helicopter was adopted in 1979. Its take-off weight is 11 tons, which makes it possible to take on ASW equipment and the means of searching for submarines (radar, sonar,

The destroyer "Byesstrashny" (434) [MoD RF]

Ka-27 helicopter, 1985 [US Navy, courtesy John Jordan]

magnetometer), and weapons such as one ASW AT 3 cal. 400 mm torpedo or two "Kolibri" cal. 330 mm torpedoes. The crew consists of two men. Top speed is 290 km/h, flight range 800 km (with a load of 700 kg), flight time 4.5 h. The Project 956 ships often sail without a helicopter, especially when operating in the coastal zone or when operating within a formation, part of which is an aircraft carrier.

Radiolocation

The ships received a relatively modern set of radiolocation equipment. In the first place, three types of "Fregat" air surveillance radars: "Fregat-M", "Fregat-M1" and "Fregat-M2". The detection range of the "Fregat" radar is approx. 200 km for a target of 5 m2 signature, flying at medium altitude, and 30 km for smaller targets. A surface target of 300 m2 signature is detected from a distance of 35 NM. The "Poima-E" computer cooperating with the radar can track up to 20 targets. Two navigation radars Vaygatch (MR-212) with a range of 40 km and antennas fitted to the main mast, below the antenna of the "Fregat" radar, are used to monitor the sea surface[11].

The radioelectronic counter-measures of the ship are radio-technical reconnaissance systems and active radio-electronic interference: "Start" (MP-401) and "Start-2" (MP-407). The decoy/dipole launchers are grouped at the stern of the ship. Launchers PK-2M (2 × 2 ZIF-121 calibre 140 mm with a reserve of 200 decoys). Two twin-barrel PK-2M launchers are designed to interfere with guided missiles heading the ship. The com-

plex includes: 2 × 2 ZIF-121-02 launchers cal. 140 mm, fire control system "Smeta", and turbo-jet rockets TSP-47, TST-47 and TSTV-47 cal. 140 mm. Starting from the eighth ship of the series, two to eight 10-rail fixed, hand-operated KT-216 launchers of the PK-10 complex ("Smelyj-P") were installed. These can fire three types of 122 mm rounds. They are used to interfere with thermal seekers and missiles guided with laser beams or television. In this way, active as well as passive electronic interference devices are included in the ships' electronic warfare systems.

The ships do not have an integrated command system. There is such a thing as a combat information centre (Russian: Boyevoy Informatsyonny Post - BIP), but this is not the place where information from ship surveillance and weapon systems automatically streams in. The control panels of individual systems are scattered all over the ship and often have no electronic connection with each other. All the problems of mutual information connection are now being solved on the modernized "Sapfir-U" plotting board, which is operated manually and shows the air and sea situation around the ship.

Other equipment

Means of communication ensure reliable, two-way radio communication of the ship with any station from any point of the world's ocean on 20 channels at the same time. They include seven short and medium wave radio stations, nine UKF and DCF radios, and also 22 KF, SF and SDF radios. Additionally, the ships are equipped with the "Printsep" satellite communication system. The navigation equipment of the ship includes: a gyro-compass, an IEL-1 log, an AP-4-956 automatic course drafting device, an NEL-M2 echosounder, the KPF-ZK and KPF-7F navigation systems, a "Rumb" radio direction-finder, the "Slyuz" space navigation systems (ADK-3M), "Parus" and "Tsitsada" and a number of others. The set is completed by the MR-212 navigation radar with three antennas.

The ship's watercraft equipment consists of: one command cutter Project 1390, one working boat Project 338M, one JLP6 boat.

Crew

In peacetime, the full-time crew of the destroyer is 296 men, including 25 officers and 48 non-commissioned officers (called "mitchmans" in Russian). During wartime, the crew increases to 358. In the opinion of Soviet specialists, the Project 956 destroyers provide comfortable accommodation for the ship's company. British officers visiting one of these destroyers in the early 1990s were less enthusiastic in their assessments. Conditions for the crew were described as bearable, though the officers' cabins received a good assessment. Officers have single and double cabins at their disposal. There are a total of 20 officers' cabins (five single ones) for 34 officers. Non-commissioned officers occupy two- and four-bed cabins (a total of 15 cabins). Naval ratings live in 16 (18) cabins, 10-25 men in each of them. There was over 3 m2 of living space per one person. The accommodation and service rooms are air-conditioned - the temperature can be adjusted from -25 to +34 ° C. Officers and non-commissioned officers have separate messes at their disposal, the crew have three canteens. In addition, the crew have at their disposal: a library, cable TV, a sports room, sanitary and medical facilities.

Modernization of the Project 956

Destroyers of the Project 956 have great modernization potential. Therefore, not surprising is the designers' willingness to use this opportunity and create a new version of the ship with improved combat capabilities, a multi-purpose ship in the full sense of the term. Conceptual work on this issue was undertaken during the construction of the series. In 1981-1982 a series of studies on the possibility of installing new weapon models was carried out. Considered were also, among others, various variants of the ship's power unit, including the possibility of converting steam turbines into gas ones. In this respect, five variants were contemplated with different arrangements and output of the power unit, with displacement ranging from 8,000 to 14,000 tons. A number of possible changes to armament were also studied.

First of all, this refers to the change in anti-submarine measures that constituted the Achilles' heel of "Sovremenny" and her sister ships. The possibilities of installing new hydroacoustic complexes were considered. The goal was to increase the detection and accuracy range as well as the reliability of identification of detected objects. A change in the aircraft equipment was also discussed, in particular the conversion of the hangar from folding to permanent one and the possibility of accommodating two helicopters. This problem is spiced up by the fact that such a possibility had existed almost from the beginning of the work on the technical project, but as one of the constructors stated, none of the sailors had raised this matter. In addition to the collective defence system, the "Uragan", from two to four self-defense gun-missile modules were to be added. In order to modernize the radiolocation means, it was planned to install a second antenna to the general surveillance radar. All these works and analyses had shown that the creation of a multi-purpose ship by equipping it with all weapon models available is a costly way to solve the problem. All the studies eventually led to the creation in the late 1980s of three modernization variants known under the codename 956U ("Usilonny", i.e. with strengthened armament).

The first variant differed from the base Project 956 in one respect, the "Moskit" complex, the SM-403 launchers were to be installed for 16 "Onix" and "Kalibr" anti-ship missiles. In the second option, instead of the aft AK-130 mm turret, it was intended to install multi-purpose hull-mounted vertical launchers 3S-14 for 16 "Onix" or "Kalibr" missiles. In the third variant of the Project 956U, only one 3S-14 aft launcher was planned for 24 missiles (also "Onix" and "Kalibr"). Fire control was to be provided by the new "Monument" complex, which was to replace the existing "Mineral" type. In addition, in all variants, beside the "Fregat-M2" radar it was intended to install the "Fregat-MA" radar and electronic warfare means. Instead of the RBU-1000 throwers and the AK-630M battery, it was intended to mount two "Kortik" modules for the first and third variant and four modules for the third variant. On 12 October 1990, a decision was made to build ships with strengthened armament and new TTR were approved. The main designer of this project was I. I. Rubis. In December 1990, all design work was done. The first variant was to be implemented by modernising already constructed ships, and the third variant was to be applied on newly-built ships. The financial crisis caused the abandonment of these plans. In 1993, work on the Project 956U were resumed, but now with a gas turbine power unit and a new set of weapons. According to this variant, it was planned to complete the hull with the construction number 880. The ship was to get 3Z-14 launchers for all types of missiles (including

The destroyer "Byespokoyny", 1998 [Jane's Fighting Ships 2000/01]

anti-ship and ASW), a permanent hangar for a helicopter and only one A-217 130 mm gun. It was all the more strange that there was only one piece of the A-217 available on the training ground. But this project, like the previous ones, collapsed for financial reasons. In 1993, another project was prepared, this time for a civilian passenger ship based on the Project 956 using hulls numbered 879 and 880. But it remained only on paper.

Operational service

The prototype ship with the class name "Sovremenny" ("Contemporary") was officially listed in the Northern Fleet on 24 January 1981. In fact, she arrived in the North only in August 1982 after the end of lengthy trials. In addition to "Sovremenny", the destroyers of the Northern Fleet were: "Otchayanny", "Otlitchny", "Byezupretchny", "Okrylennj", "Gremyashtchy" (ex-"Vedushtchy"), "Rastoropny", "Byezuderzhny" and "Byesstrashny". The Pacific Ocean Fleet was reinforced by: "Osmotritelny", "Boyevoy", "Stoyky", "Burny", "Bystry" and "Byezboyaznenny", and the Baltic Fleet: "Byespokoyny" and "Nastoytchyvy" ("Moskovskyi Komsomolets"). Directing of the majority of the ships to the two oceanic fleets resulted from the size of these ships and their seaworthiness that work perfectly in difficult hydrometeorological conditions. Unfortunately, their power units designed to facilitate their operation and reduce cost, have become their curse. Problems with boilers meant that instead the predicted minimum of 20-year period of service, they were operated for much shorter time. Most of them were in service for less than 10 years! For example, "Sovremenny" after eight years arrived at the shipyard, from where she went to scrap. The same happened to other ships of this type: "Otchayanny" was actively operated for 10 years, "Otlitchny" - 11 years, "Osmotritelnj" 7 years, "Byezupretchny" - 8 years, "Stoyky" - 5 years, "Okrylanny" - 6 years, "Gremyashtchy" - 8 years, "Bystry" - 9 years, "Rastoro-

pny" - 8 years, "Byezboyaznenny" - 9 years, "Byezuderzhny" - 7 years[12]. On 30 September 1998, six destroyers were simultaneously written off: "Okrilenny", "Otlitchny", "Osmotritelny", "Otchayanny", "Sovremenny", "Stoyky". After a few years break on 20 July 2001, "Byezupretchny" was sent for scrap. On 18 December 2006, "Gremyashtchy" ended her service. On 1 December 2010 "Boyevy" left the navy. On 8 August 2012 goodbye was said to "Rostoropny", and in December to "Byezuderzhny". The unfinished "Vnushitelny" was removed from the fleet list in 1987, it was further used as a floating depot at the Nikolaev shipyard, and in 1996 it was sent for scrap. Currently, there are only six of the 17 ships of this type in the line ("Burny", "Byespokoyny", "Nastoytchyvy", "Admiral Ushakov", "Bystry" and "Byezboayznenny"). The youngest destroyer of the series - "Byesstrashny" (handed over to the fleet on 30 December 1993) - changed her name to "Admiral Ushakov" (17 April 2004). The destroyers "Bystryj" and "Burnyj" are undergoing major overhaul at Dalzavod. "Nastoytchyvy" performs a role of the flagship of the Baltic Fleet. "Byespokoyny" and "Byezboyaznenny" are in reserve.

Evaluation

The destroyer Project 956 was designed and built in the Cold War era, having taken into account the presence on the oceans of its main opponent - the American multirole destroyer of the Spruance type. The Soviet admirals wanted it to be not inferior than "the American". The first difference that strikes the eye is the power unit. The US ship is powered by gas turbines with better specifications and greater reliability. More importantly, the US drive unit can reach its full output after just 20 minutes, while the Soviet one needs 1.5 hours for it. However, the main disadvantage of the Soviet power unit was the demand for high quality boiler water, which often led to boiler failures and complicated the operation of all main mechanisms. As it turned out, the Soviet (and later Russian) navy technically and organizationally was not prepared for intensive operation of a power unit with high-pressure boilers. This circumstance determined the fate of the entire series, which quickly disappeared from the seas and oceans. Other disadvantages include the following: the presence of only one radiolocation station for general surveillance, which at the same time was the channel of targeting for the "Uragan" complex, which made the air defence system quite sensitive (with a large radiolocation echo already mentioned). Without a doubt, the Sovremenny type had a decisive advantage when it came to gunfire. Within four minutes the destroyer's guns are capable of firing over 6,000 kg of lethal metal at the enemy (cruiser Project 68bis only 4,950 kg, but the piercing force of its 152 millimetre rounds was obviously greater).

The US equivalent beats it with the ASW strength. The initial advantage of Project 956 in missile weaponry disappeared with the modernization of the Spruance type ships and equipping them with multi-purpose launchers and "Tomahawk" missiles, which has given them a clear advantage over their Soviet counterpart.

Broadside callsigns of the "Sovremenny" type destroyers:

"Byezboyaznenny": 672 (1990), 711 (1992); 754 (1993)

"Byezuderzhny": 682 (1991), 444 (1992), 435 (1993), 406 (1994)

"Byezupretchny": 820 (1985), 430 (1986), 681 (1987), 459 (1987), 413 (1990), 417 (1994), 439 (1995)

"Byespokoyny": 678 (1986), 620 (1993)

"Byesstrashny": 694 (1993), 678 (1995), 434 (1996), 474 (2016)

"Boyevoy": 678 (1986), 640 (20.12.1987), 728 (1989), 770 (1990), 720 (1993)

"Burny": 677 (1988), 795 (1989), 722 (1990), 778 (1994)

"Bystry" 676 (1989), 786 (1991), 715 (1993)

"Vazhny": 698 (1999)

"Vyedushtchy": 680 (1988), 684 (1989), 605 (1990), 420 (1990), 739 (1991), 439 (1991), 429 (1995), 404 (2005)

"Vyetchny" (building number 892): 698 (2006)

"Vdumtchivy": 690 (2000)

"Vnushitelny" (nr bud 891): 693 (2005)

"Moskovskyi Komsomolets": 675 (1992), 610 (1993), 810 (1994), 610 (1996)

"Okryllenny": 670 (1986), 424 (1988), 444 (1990), 415 (1996)

"Osmotritelny": 672 (1984), 780 (1986), 755 (1986), 730 (1992), 735 (1993), 730 (1997)

"Otlitchny": 671 (1983), 403 (1985), 434 (1988), 408 (1990), 151 (1991), 474 (1992)

"Otchayanny": 431 (1981), 684 (1982), 460 (1984), 405 (1987), 417 (1990), 433 (1990), 475 (1991), 441, 417 (1998)

"Rastoropny": 520?, 447 (1989), 673 (1990), 633 (1990), 400 (1992), 420 (1993)

"Sovremenny": 670 (1980), 760 (1981), 618 (1982), 680 (1982), 402 (1982), 441 (1984), 431 (19880, 420 (1990), 402 (1992), 431 (1998), 753?

"Stoyky": 679 (1986), 645 (1987), 719 (1989), 727 (1990), 743 (1993)

Bibliography

Apalkov J. V., "Udarnye korabli", Moscow 2008.

Burov V. N., "Otetchestvennoye varnoye korablestroyene v tretem stoleti svoyey istori", St. Petersburg 1995.

Kinski A., "Rosyjskie niszczyciele rakietowe projektu 956", Part 1 and 2, "Nowa Technika Wojskowa" 1995, Issue No. 11-12.

Kuzin V. P., Nikolskyi V. I., "Voyenno-Morskoy Flot SSSR 1945-1991", St. Petersburg 1996.

Ovsyannikov S. I., Spiridopulo V. I., "Sovetsky superesminets tretyego pokolenya", Parts. 1, 2, 3 [in:] "Istorya Korabla" 2004, Issue No. 1-2; 2005.

Pavlov A. S., "Esmintsy pervogo ranka", Yakutsk 2000.

Platonov A. V., "Sovetske minonostsy", St. Petersburg 2003.

Edited by V. E. Yuchnin, "Poslednyi eskadrenny minononosets VMF SSSR", St. Petersburg 2001.

Schielle M., "Współczesny 'Nowoczesny'", "Przegląd Morski"" 2000, Issue No. 2.

Shirokorad A., "Sovetskaya korabelnaya artillerya", St. Petersburg 1996.

Śmigielski A., "Wielkie niszczyciele rakietowe typu Sowriemiennyj", "Morze" 1991, Issue No. 5.

"Morskoy Sbornik", Issues 1995-2002.

"Nevskyi Bastion", Issues 1999-2005.

Endnotes

1. The calculations carried out by operational officers of the USSR Navy showed that the ships until they were destroyed (10-15 minutes) would be able to eliminate the tracked aircraft carrier with a probability of 0.5 to 0.85. At the same time, the Project 26 bis cruisers were the most effective, with 180 mm guns were equipped with not only HE rounds but also nuclear ones.

2. A.S. Pavlov, "Esmintsy pyervogo ranga", Yakutsk 2003, p.3

3. According to A. S. Pavlov, Admiral Gorshkov personally made the decision to design a twin-barrel automatic gun for large ships on its base. In this way, "automatically" the rate of fire 90 rounds/min. would be achieved.

4. Missile cruisers and large anti-submarine warships received 4-digit code numbers: 1144, 1164 and 1155 in accordance with the design numbers of the previous generation of the 1134, 1134A, 1134B and 1135 ships developed in the 1960s. As a prototype of the design number for the new destroyer among the ships of the second generation did not exist, a rather original decision was made to accept the number 56, and to indicate that it was a third generation ship, it was decided that the first digit would be accepted from the third generation of nuclear submarines - the number "9". The code "Sarytch" was taken from the family of predatory birds similarly to projects 1134A "Byerkut", 1135 "Buryevestnik".

5. Incidentally, it should be added that after the decision of the Council of Ministers of the USSR of 28 April 1962, a design office was created in the CNII that issued expert opinions in the field of naval architecture. It must be admitted that in this respect Soviet ships beat the heads of their western counterparts.

6. The dimensions of the ship were largely determined by the conditions of the "A. A. Zhdanov" Shipyard, which could not build ships longer than 140-150 m due to the limited size of the slipway.

7. A. Śmigielski, *Wielkie niszczyciele rakietowe typu Sowremiennyj*, "Morze" 1991, Issue No. 5.

8. According to the designers, the creation of a detection system that doubled the basic ship's air surveillance station would lead to unnecessary costs and increase the weight of the complex.

9. The automatic 130 mm L/70 multi-purpose gun according to Swedish sources was developed based on documentation of similar Bofors guns of 120 mm calibre, which was obtained by Soviet intelligence in the early 70s (see A. Śmigielski ..., op. cit.).

10. In the summer of 1986, during the acceptance tests of the destroyer "Boyevoy" (the sixth in the series), the ship's capability to lay mines was checked. For this purpose, the destroyer got four types of mines – UKSM anchor mine, UDM-500 bottom mine, jet-emerging RM-2G and anti-submarine RM-2G mine-missiles, which she laid on the fleet range in the Liepaja area.

11. A. Kiński, *Rosyjskie niszczyciele rakietowe projektu 956*, Part 2 [in:] "Nowa Technika Wojskowa" 1995, Issue No. 12, p. 45.

12. A. V. Platonov, *Sovyetskye minonostsy*, Part 2, St. Petersburg 2003, p. 77.

Spravedlivyy

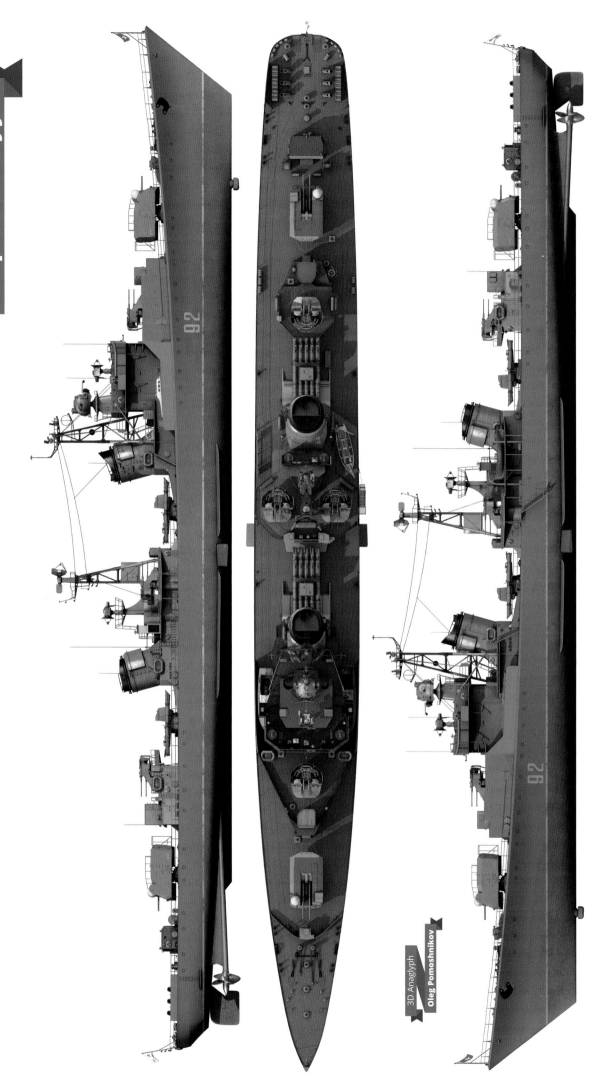

3D Anaglyph
Oleg Pomoshnikov